CONTENT

The MIT Press Essential Knowledge series

A complete list of the titles in this series appears at the back of this book.

CONTENT

KATE EICHHORN

The MIT Press | Cambridge, Massachusetts | London, England

The MIT Press would like to thank the anonymous peer reviewers who provided comments on drafts of this book. The generous work of academic experts is essential for establishing the authority and quality of our publications. We acknowledge with gratitude the contributions of these otherwise uncredited readers.

This book was set in Chaparral Pro by New Best-set Typesetters Ltd. Printed and bound in the United States of America.

Library of Congress Cataloging-in-Publication Data

Names: Eichhorn, Kate, 1971- author.
Title: Content / Kate Eichhorn.
Description: Cambridge : The MIT Press, 2022. | Series: The MIT press essential knowledge series | Includes bibliographical references and index.
Identifiers: LCCN 2021000773 | ISBN 9780262543286 (paperback)
Subjects: LCSH: Information services industry. | Online social networks. | Search engines. | Internet—Social aspects. | Internet—Psychological aspects. | Information technology—Psychological aspects.
Classification: LCC HD9999.I492 E33 2022 | DDC 302.2/402854678—dc23
LC record available at https://lccn.loc.gov/2021000773

10 9 8 7 6 5 4 3 2 1

CONTENTS

Series Foreword   vii

Preface   ix

1   A Brief History of Content in a Digital Era   1

2   User-Generated Content   31

3   Content Farms   57

4   Content Capital   79

5   Journalism and Politics after Content   103

6   Content Automation   129

Glossary   145

Notes   151

Further Reading   159

Index   161

SERIES FOREWORD

The MIT Press Essential Knowledge series offers accessible, concise, beautifully produced pocket-size books on topics of current interest. Written by leading thinkers, the books in this series deliver expert overviews of subjects that range from the cultural and the historical to the scientific and the technical.

In this era of instant information gratification, we have ready access to opinions, rationalizations, and superficial descriptions. Much harder to come by is the foundational knowledge that informs a principled understanding of the world. Essential Knowledge books fill that need. Synthesizing specialized subject matter for nonspecialists and engaging critical topics through fundamentals, each of these compact volumes offers readers a point of access to complex ideas.

When nearly everyone in the United States and around the world was being asked to shelter in place at the start of the COVID-19 pandemic in April 2020, Florida's governor Ron DeSantis held a press conference to address what he perceived to be a serious problem—the lack of new content. "People have been starved for content," he said. "We haven't had a lot of new content since the beginning of March . . . we need to support content, especially sports." On this basis, DeSantis declared that alongside medical personnel and employees working at pharmacies and grocery stores, employees of professional sports and media production companies could return to work and start producing new content.

To rationalize his positioning of content as an essential service, DeSantis appealed to both history and psychology. First, he observed, "We've never had a period like this in modern American history where you've had such little new content, particularly in the sporting realm. I mean, people are watching, we're watching, like, reruns from the early 2000s, watching Tom Brady do the Super Bowl then." Second, he speculated, content might ease the pain of people who are "chomping at the bit," and even have a positive psychological impact: "To be able to have some light at the end of the tunnel . . . see that things may get back on a better course—I think from just a psychological perspective I think is a good thing." While DeSantis's press conference garnered considerable attention, his claims provoked many questions.

DeSantis didn't define "modern American history," but even if he were referencing a relatively short period—let's say, 2010 to 2020—his statement about the unprecedented lack of content in the midst of the COVID-19 lockdown was certainly false. By all accounts, we're producing much more content now than we were just a few years ago, so even a significant disruption in content production would be unlikely to leave us with less new content than any other time in "modern American history." By one estimate, as of 2020, the world was producing 44 zettabytes of data (or $1,000^7$ bytes) annually—an estimated ten times the amount of data we were turning out in 2013.[1] Depending on how you define *content* (a task easier said than done), content and data aren't interchangeable terms. Still, the growing amount of data in the world is by no means disconnected from the explosion of content production. And, during the COVID-19 lockdown, content production didn't decrease; as billions of people around the world found themselves stranded at home, the production of content surged alongside the demand for it. On the one hand, established sites from Facebook to YouTube saw significant spikes in traffic as the lockdown was imposed. Several newer and less well-known content providers and platforms also experienced growth during this period as people who normally do their work in person (e.g., yoga instructors, history professors, professional musicians, and so on) searched for viable ways to produce and share content online.[2]

However, DeSantis didn't simply claim that we were witnessing an unprecedented decline in content. He also claimed that content should be viewed as an essential service—something vital to Floridians' health and wellness—for psychological reasons. At least some Florida residents and businesses appeared to agree with him on this. The World Wrestling Federation (WWF), which records its *Monday Night Raw* programs from a studio in Orlando, even echoed the governor's suggestion that new content would have a positive psychological impact. As one WWF spokesperson echoed, "WWF and its Superstars bring families together and deliver a sense of hope, determination and perseverance."[3] Still, many onlookers were left wondering why content, including the type of content produced by the WWF, was being considered essential during a pandemic. After all, no evidence suggests that new content necessarily promotes hope or resilience. Yet at least some evidence suggests that excessive screen time, which generally includes consumption of new content, may have detrimental effects.[4]

As someone who happened to be finishing a book about content at the time of DeSantis's press conference,

I was also left with a few additional questions. How could DeSantis claim that we've never before had a period of modern history with so little content when the concept of content is itself relatively recent? What turn of events had led an elected government official to view content production as essential—something essential enough to be prioritized alongside access to food or health services? And how could something so ambiguously defined and misunderstood be positioned as vital to our ability to carry on in the face of adversity?

DeSantis's press conference may have been one of the more absurd episodes to unfold on the political stage during the COVID-19 crisis, but for the purposes of this book, it is by no means insignificant. While he was certainly wrong to conclude that "we've never had a period like this in modern American history" and likely wrong to argue a positive correlation between new content and psychological wellbeing, he may have gotten one thing right—in our content-rich world, there at least appears to be a constant demand for new content.

We no longer live in a world where newspapers arrive on our doorstep once a day. Many people now expect news updates all day long. Likewise, television isn't something we tune in to on certain days of the week at certain times to watch certain episodes. Many people expect to have access to new content on streaming platforms like Netflix and Hulu on a constant basis. The same holds true for the content we produce ourselves. Imagine how disconcerted we would be to wake up and log on to Facebook, Twitter, or Instagram and find not a single new update. After all, absent a truly apocalyptic event, when would we ever wake up and find no new content posted on our social media accounts? Like it or not, content has become an integral part of our lives. Many people even expect new content 24/7 and 365 days of the year. But what exactly is content? Who produces it? Why and how did it come to be viewed as "essential"? And how will content continue to structure our economy, culture, politics, and everyday lives in the future? These are the questions this book explores and, where possible, answers.

Like any book, this one is the result of many conversations carried out over a period of several years. First, I'm grateful to J.K. who shared with me his expertise on search engine optimization and web entrepreneurship, and eventually, his moral and ethical reservations about the content industry. Without his insights, this book never would have been written. I also wish to thank media historian Craig Robertson who invited me to participate on a panel about the concept of information at a meeting of the Society of Cinema and Media Studies in 2018. On the panel, I noticed that although the term *content* was seeping into our conversation, none of us—all researchers in the field of media studies or information studies—appeared prepared to define it or to fully explicate its relationship to the word *information*. This affirmed my suspicion that the concept merited additional critical attention. Since then, this short book has benefited from several other conversations and contributions. Special thanks to Eli Recht-Appel and Jackson Pacheco for their research assistance and insights. In early August 2020, I had an opportunity to discuss this book for the first time at an event organized by Marcus Boon, and I thank Marcus, his students, and the other participants for their questions and suggestions on how to expand the book's scope and depth. This book also benefited from three close readings by anonymous reviewers who offered precise and at times conflicting feedback on how to make it a better book. I hope I was able to address at least some of their broad concerns. Finally, I wish to thank the editors, designers, and publicists at the MIT Press, especially Erika Barrios for her assistance, Matthew Abbate for his editorial feedback, and Gita Devi Manaktala for acquiring this title and seeing it through the press.

A BRIEF HISTORY OF CONTENT IN A DIGITAL ERA

Like water or air, content is ubiquitous. But unlike these natural elements, content can't be easily defined. After all, content doesn't have any notable characteristics. Perhaps more important, unlike water and air—at least, clean water and breathable air—which are both depleting resources, content is not at risk. In the twenty-first century, content appears to possess infinite potential to keep expanding. But if content is as ubiquitous as it appears to be, what is it, and what are the parameters of the industry that supports its growth and seems to know no bounds?

Defining Content in a Digital Era

According to the *Oxford English Dictionary*, content is "that which is contained in anything." Logically, then, *content* can refer to socks in a drawer, books in a box, or sand in an hourglass. But none of these material objects are of concern in the content industry. By default, in the content industry, *content* implicitly points to digital, not physical, materials. But still, little consensus exists about what the term means, even in this more narrowly defined context. The second edition of the *Oxford Dictionary of the Internet* defines *content* as "The information found in a Web site and the way in which it is structured." Similarly, Merriam-Webster's defines *content* as "the principal substance (such as written matter, illustrations, or music) offered by a website." While these two definitions are partially correct, neither is sufficiently inclusive.

First, digital content is no longer, strictly speaking, found only on websites. After all, mobile apps such as Snapchat and Instagram also generate and circulate content. Second, eliding *content* with *information* is misleading. Information is generally equated with imparting knowledge, but as anyone who has ever spent time online appreciates, a lot of content in circulation doesn't impart any knowledge at all. To illustrate, consider the case of the "Instagram egg."

In early 2019, the most-liked image on Instagram was a digital photograph of a brown egg on a white background. As of March 2019, the egg (originally just a stock photo) had already accrued more than 50 million likes. While the egg, which would eventually be widely known as the Instagram egg, certainly constitutes content, can it be easily classified as information or knowledge? Since it was circulating on Instagram solely for the purpose of becoming the most-liked image on the social media platform and not to convey a message or share information or tell a story of any kind, the egg arguably reveals a great deal about the essence of content in a digital era. Certainly, some content does convey a message, share information, or tell a story, but content isn't obliged to fulfill any of these goals. Content, as demonstrated by the Instagram egg, may circulate solely for the purpose of circulating. What has changed with the arrival of the content industry is both simple and significant.

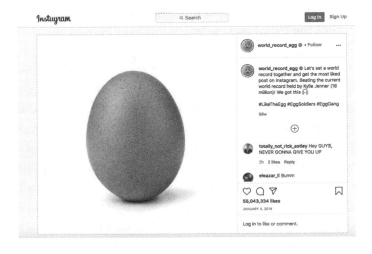

Figure 1 The "Instagram egg," posted by @world_record_egg in early 2019.

As political scientist Jodi Dean argues in *Democracy and Other Neoliberal Fantasies: Communicative Capitalism and Left Politics*, in a digital era, "the exchange value of messages overcomes their use value." In other words, messages are no longer primarily sent from senders to receivers. Part of a circulating stream of data, a message's particular content is irrelevant, but so is the need that it be received. As Dean notes, "The only thing that is relevant is circulation, the addition to the pool."[1] Hence the existence of the Instagram egg. The Instagram egg could have been a kitten or blender or hockey stick, and anyone could have sent or liked the image. What mattered was not what the Instagram egg had to communicate or to whom but that it was circulating at all, and this is arguably what makes the Instagram egg such an exemplary example of content.

The Instagram egg may be notorious, but it is not an outlier. Indeed, in many respects, it epitomizes content—the raw material of the content industry. What made the Instagram egg stand out wasn't what it communicated but rather what it did, and what it did was simply circulate widely. This is precisely why economist Bharat Anand, author of *The Content Trap*, argues that in an age of content, the most successful companies aren't those that produce or sell great content but rather those that simply facilitate its management or circulation.[2] This focus is what seems to separate content and the content industry from earlier forms of cultural erosion. One might ask, after all, aren't content and the content industry simply an extension of a culture industry that has existed since at least the rise of mass media? Like the culture industry described in disparaging terms by critical theorists Theodor Adorno and Max Horkheimer in the late 1940s, the content industry is also an industry defined by repetition—one where "characteristic innovations are never anything more than improvements of mass reproduction" and consumers are "directed to the technique, and not to the contents—which are stubbornly repeated, outworn, and by now half-discredited."[3] Of course, in the culture industry described by Adorno and Horkheimer, amusement and entertainment still existed. Even if trite and trivial, or worse yet, dangerously merging the boundary between culture and pure amusement, the images in circulation were still doing and communicating something. Can the same be said of the Instagram egg? Again, the Instagram egg isn't culture or amusement or even an advertisement for eggs.

If one takes the Instagram egg as a sort of quintessential example of content—something that circulates for the sake of circulation—one key question remains, which is why and how nearly everything that circulates digitally came to be known as *content*? Before the rise of the content industry, content already had a specific meaning in both legal discourses (specifically, in relation to copyright law) and marketing. To fully appreciate how the concept became so widely adopted and eventually accrued its current connotations, we need to investigate the term's slow but steady uptake in the 1990s to early 2000s.

The Rise of the Content Industry

The first reference to the content industry in the *New York Times* appeared in a 1998 article by William Safire. In "The Summer of This Content," Safire observes, "If any word in the English language is hot, buzzworthy and finger-snappingly with-it, surpassing even millennium in both general discourse and insider-ese, that word is content." Safire's article goes on to offer a short history of content and the content industry, beginning with John P. Noon's decision to trademark the term *content* in 1991. According to Safire, Noon decided to trademark the term because his enterprise, Content World Publishing, was planning to launch a new magazine called *Content* that, in Noon's words, would be "geared toward people in the content industry" and explore "how different types of content can make it into digital media."[4]

If Noon's mandate to explore "how different types of content can make it into digital media" sounds vague, it likely reflects the fact that in 1991 few people had any reference point for digital media, let alone content. But this is not surprising. The first web browser launched in 1990, but it would take several years for anything resembling the modern web to even begin to take form.

Sadly, Noon was detrimentally ahead of his time. In 1991, little market existed for a magazine targeting the content industry. Even a decade later, when Noon launched the Content World Trade Show, the industry was still in a nascent form. While Noon's trade show initially attracted over a thousand attendees, by July 2004 *Computer World* reported that the trade show had been canceled due to declining interest and attendance. The same article reported that Noon was selling off many of his content-related assets, which included the Content.net and Contentmanagement.com domains. Ironically, just as Noon was winding down the Content World Trade Show and selling off his domains, the content industry he had envisioned in the early 1990s was about to explode.

To be clear, the content industry—an umbrella term for all types of companies in the business of owning or providing digital content of any kind, from text publications to music to movies—was already taking shape in the 1990s. However, the growth of an industry that rests on the creation and circulation of content was initially slowed by several factors.

Inadequate Search Engines
In an era when *search* was not yet synonymous with *Google*, many search engines were available (e.g., AltaVista, Ask

Jeeves, Excite, Lycos, and WebCrawler), but they were semifunctional at best. One could put content online, but there was no obvious way to ensure it would ever be found.

Limited File-Sharing Options and Slow Internet Speeds
Unless you were an established media outlet with many resources, throughout the 1990s and into the early 2000s, the types of content you could share online were limited. Without platforms like YouTube and Vimeo, for example, sharing video files was phenomenally difficult. Without affordable website development platforms, such as Word-Press, even building a website and posting textual content online generally required a lot of time and expertise. But as a wider variety of content started to appear online, including streamed music and videos, other technical challenges remained. In the 1990s, most people still relied on dial-up internet. At top speeds, dial-up could stream about 56 kilobytes per second. As a result, early web users often spent a lot of time just waiting for basic websites to load. Downloading any type of file with more information—for example, a video—would have been impossible, or at least extremely onerous. With a maximum download speed of 56 kilobytes per second, it would take over a week to download an average-length feature film. Thus, even in the early 2000s, the types of content one could easily post and put into circulation were limited at best.

Limited User-Generated Content

Another factor that limited the content industry's growth in the 1990s was the small amount of user-generated content. While such content existed in the 1990s, it was available on a much smaller scale than today. In the early years of the web, GeoCities (1995) offered a somewhat clunky but possible way to build and launch a personal website, though users needed at least a basic knowledge of HTML to use the platform. Later, both Blogger (1999) and LiveJournal (1999) launched to offer more accessible ways for people to share their ideas online, even if they didn't know how to code a site. But in the early days of GeoCities, Blogger, and LiveJournal, user-generated content was limited. Platforms that would later facilitate the production and circulation of user-generated content in other mediums (e.g., video-sharing sites such as YouTube, Vimeo, and Flickr) had yet to launch in the 1990s.

Restricted Ability to Work and Hire Remotely

At this time, producing content generally required hiring individuals with the skills to do so. Finding a few local skilled workers has always been easy, while finding hundreds or thousands of skilled workers has always necessitated casting one's search wider. Hiring far-flung employees with the needed skills was difficult in the 1990s to early 2000s because the conditions and platforms that would eventually support the massive expansion of remote work and online hiring—including online work collaboration tools such as Dropbox and Google Docs, and online hiring recruitment sites, including Elance and ODesk (now Upwork)—did not yet exist.

Limited Opportunities for Monetization

One of the main reasons the content industry didn't immediately explode as the web expanded was economic. Until the early 2000s, if domain owners wanted to run advertisements on their website, they had to sell advertising space. The process was similar to that of selling advertising space in a print publication; the only difference was that rather than selling a block of a printed page, what was now up for grabs was a bit of space on a website. Of course, in the early years of the web, domain owners needed the resources and staff to go out and attract potential advertisers in order to sell any advertising space. As a result, even if a domain owner could generate a lot of content, finding ways to make a site generate revenue remained a challenge and was only truly possible for established content providers such as large newspapers and existing media companies.

Around 2004, just as Noon appeared to be throwing in the towel, a convergence of new technologies, platforms, and products created the conditions needed for the content industry to finally expand.

Content Became Searchable

Until at least the early 2000s, the web was a rapidly evolving space but one with a chronic problem—it was an ever-expanding repository of information with no efficient search function. In 1994, the editors of *Postmodern Culture*, one of the first academic journals to start publishing on the web, were concerned enough about this new medium to warn their readers that venturing onto the web, which had grown from an estimated 100 sites in June to over 600 sites by December 1993, may result in "a kind of informational vertigo."[5] While this warning may now strike readers as hilarious, it is worth noting that for much of the 1990s, finding anything on the web was a problem. It would take nearly a decade for this problem to resolve. As search engines were refined and became more functional, however, the drive to "game the system" also increased. And more individuals and organizations started to produce content for the web that had one sole purpose: to rank high in any search. So-called discoverability came to dictate why a lot of content was being produced.

Internet Speeds Accelerated

Just as finding content got a lot easier, internet speeds started to speed up. A Pew Research Center study found that in 2000, about half of US adults were online, but only 3 percent had broadband access—the other 97 percent were still using dial-up. Dial-up usage peaked a couple of years later, but by 2003 to 2004, dial-up was in a steady and rapid decline as both new and established users embraced high-speed alternatives.[6] Accelerated internet speeds allowed people to access more content more quickly. Whether this increased the desire for content is unclear, but faster internet speeds certainly made accessing content online less tedious. Eventually, the event of "going online" would become a seamlessly integrated practice of everyday life.

Content Diversified
While the web was at first a primarily text-based medium, as internet speeds increased, music-sharing sites such as Napster and video-sharing sites such as YouTube were launched, diversifying the type of content available. Increasingly, the web was also where one went to share photographs, videos, and music files.

The Era of Social Media Arrived
In the early 2000s, social media expanded beyond the handful of sites such as GeoCities, Blogger, and LiveJournal. In the span of five years, dozens of major social media sites—some still in existence and others now defunct—appeared, including MySpace (2003), Del.icio.us (2003), Flickr (2004), Facebook (2004), YouTube (2005), Twitter (2006), and Tumblr (2007). During these years, user-

generated content and the content industry started to grow at an unprecedented rate.

Simultaneous to these technological changes, which essentially helped make the production and sharing of digital content easier and more accessible to a wider range of users, three other important things happened.

The Rise of Remote Work and the Gig Economy

First, in the late 1990s to early 2000s, the way we work went through a radical shift. For example, remote hiring sites such as Elance (1999) and ODesk (2003) appeared, enabling employers to hire workers en masse. Employers in developed nations were able to more easily outsource large-scale programming, web development, and content production projects to people anywhere in the world, including in emerging economies where highly skilled labor can often can be accessed at a fraction of the cost. During this period, online collaborative working tools also started to emerge to make remote work—and even remote collaborative projects—easier. These tools included Writely, which was launched by Upstartle in 2005, but within a year was acquired by Google and relaunched as Google Docs.

The Automation of Advertising

In 2004, Google launched a new vertical product that would transform advertising by enabling anyone who owned a domain and had a website with at least some content to generate income via automatically placed advertisements. Known as AdSense, the product was arguably the single most important factor in the content industry's expansion in the first decade of the new millennium (as discussed in chapter 3). With AdSense, the more content one had on a website, the more money one could make. Hence, at least for web entrepreneurs, the need for content, especially original *search-engine-optimized* content, soared.

Hardware Companies Started Using Free Content to Drive Sales

Finally, in the early 2000s, tech companies started to use content—namely, free content—to drive the sales of new products. After all, would smart phones have taken off as quickly as they did if there wasn't a lot of free content available online? Would many people have felt compelled to purchase a Blackberry or iPhone in 2008 if most of the content online was behind a paywall? Free content became essential to creating a perceived need for everything from smart phones to tablets to portable computers. Simply put, content created needs that might never have existed otherwise.

So, what is the content industry? In essence, it is an industry that generates revenue from the production and/ or circulation of content alone. The content in question sometimes conveys information, tells a story, or entertains, but it doesn't need to do any of these things to circulate effectively as content (again, consider the Instagram Egg). While some content is produced by paid workers, much of the content that generates income in the industry is user-generated (produced for free by users). While the content industry may be a relatively new phenomenon—one conceived of as the internet started to enter our everyday lives in the 1990s and fully realized in the first decade of the new millennium—a few theorists saw it coming as early as the 1970s.

Predictions about the Rise of the Content Industry

The content industry existed as a possibility long before it was established or named. Philosophers Theodor Adorno and Max Horkheimer saw the writing on the wall in the late 1940s. They argued at the time that the culture industry's content was already "merely a faded foreground." When one encounters the culture industry's content, such as a typical Hollywood film, what sinks in isn't a specific image or message but rather "the automated succession of standardized operations." For Adorno and Horkheimer, the culture industry's content was monotonous—an example of the rhythm of the factory floor invading culture. In their essay "The Culture Industry," Adorno and

Horkheimer accurately foresaw the growing entanglement between the culture and advertising industries and the negative consequences of this convergence.[7] What they didn't fully foresee is the extent to which the culture industry's products wouldn't simply mirror the monotonous rhythms of the factory floor but would become its raw material.

The earliest and arguably most accurate anticipation of something resembling the contemporary content industry was articulated over twenty-five years later by French philosopher Jean-François Lyotard. While serving as a visiting researcher at the University of Montreal in the late 1970s, Lyotard wrote *The Postmodern Condition: A Report on Knowledge* (published in 1979). *The Postmodern Condition* was a "report" in the traditional sense, as it was commissioned by the Conseil des universités du Québec; we might presume it was one of the conditions of Lyotard's visiting professorship. What Lyotard produced wasn't just another report destined to rot away in a government filing cabinet; *The Postmodern Condition* helped define the postmodern era. Specifically, the report laid the groundwork for understanding the status of knowledge in computerized societies.

While Lyotard never used the term *content industry* in his report and never even adopted the term *content* to describe digital information, he more or less accurately forecast the rise of the content industry. To begin, he observed that technological transformations—by which he was primarily referring to computerization—"can be expected to have a considerable impact on knowledge." He observed, "Knowledge is and will be produced in order to be sold, it is and will be consumed in order to be valorized in a new production: in both cases, the goal is exchange. Knowledge ceases to be an end in itself, it loses its 'use-value.'" Not only did Lyotard anticipate an era in which knowledge would lose its "use-value" and exist only to be exchanged, but he also accurately predicted "that the nation-states will one day fight for control of information, just as they battled in the past for control over territory."[8]

In the context of his discussion, Lyotard further predicted that as knowledge becomes an "informational commodity," the dichotomy between knowledge and ignorance would also break down. In its wake, we would witness a new divide—the difference between *payment knowledge* and *investment knowledge*. Payment knowledge, he suggested, will be exchanged for pure survival (i.e., for consumption), while investment knowledge will be exchanged to optimize the performance of other endeavors. In today's data-driven culture, payment knowledge is arguably the type of data we share on a daily basis to carry out quotidian tasks—for example, entering a building or logging into an online bank account. Investment knowledge refers to all the other data we exchange on a daily basis (e.g., the data we share when we decide to use a fitness app that tracks our steps or when we post photographs on a social media platform like Instagram). On its own, the information we share with an app like Fitbit or a photograph we share on Instagram isn't valuable at all. But when a company has access to millions of users' daily step counts or millions of photographs, it has something that is highly valuable. This investment knowledge (what most people would now simply call data) can be used to optimize other projects. To illustrate, consider what happens when you're asked to upload an image of yourself to a digital platform. On its own, your photograph isn't valuable. If a platform has millions of tagged photographs just like yours, however, the photographs can be mined and, in turn, used to drive research and development. (As an example, Facebook used its trove of tagged user photographs to drive research and development on facial recognition technologies.)

Finally, despite being preoccupied with how the emerging era of the informational commodity would impact nation-states, Lyotard also recognized that in the future, nation-states might yield considerably less power than multinational technology companies. Early in his report on knowledge, he speculates:

Already in the last few decades, economic powers have reached the point of imperiling the stability of the State through new forms of the circulation of capital that go by the generic name of *multi-national corporations*. These new forms of circulation imply that investment decisions have, at least in part, passed beyond the control of the nation-states. The question threatens to become even more thorny with the development of computer technology and telematics. Suppose, for example, that a firm such as IBM is authorized to occupy a belt in the earth's orbital field and launch communications satellites or satellites housing data banks. Who will have access to them? Who will determine which channels or data are forbidden? The State? Or will the State simply be one user among others? New legal issues will be raised, and with them the question: "who will know?"[9]

Four decades later, one conclusion seems to be that in many respects, states have become one user among others. What Lyotard could not have fully predicted in the late 1970s was that by the 2000s, IBM would be just one of the many multinationals yielding revenues in excess of most nation-states' GNPs.

Throughout the 1980s and 1990s, Lyotard's ideas gained currency, especially his premise that knowledge itself would increasingly circulate as an "informational commodity" divorced from its use value. By the end of the twentieth century, critical theorists and economists alike recognized that this was happening and would have widespread consequences. Not until the mid-aughts did the emerging use of the term *content* start to receive critical attention.

One of the earliest indications that we might want to approach the new use of the term *content* with a dose of skepticism appeared in cultural critic McKenzie Wark's 2006 book *A Hacker Manifesto*. As Wark wrote at the time, "Privatizing information and knowledge as commodified 'content' distorts and deforms its free development, and prevents the very concept of its freedom from its own free development." Wark further observed, "Workers and hackers have in common an interest in resisting educational 'content' that merely trains slaves for commodity production, but also in resisting the inroads the vectoralist class wishes to make into education as an industry."[10] The decision to at least periodically place *content* in scare quotes throughout *A Hacker Manifesto* was most likely not a coincidence. It suggests, at the very least, a wariness about the term's emerging currency in the capitalist economy under critique in the book.

In many respects, though, Wark's apprehension about uncritically adopting the term *content* has remained an exception to the rule. As the term grew more ubiquitous in the first two decades of the twenty-first century, critical dialogues about content—what it means in a digital era and its adoption and circulation across industries and disciplines—have remained surprisingly rare. This brings me back to the central question of this book: What is content?

To begin, content isn't necessarily data, even if the two terms are frequently used interchangeably. Some argue that this is because content is contextualized information and data is not. Others argue that while content conveys a message (in words or images or sound), data does not. But as suggested earlier in this chapter, some content—for example, the Instagram egg—seems to exist simply for the sake of circulation alone and not to convey a message. Given such vexing problems, attempts to define content seem to lead to only the most imperfect operational definitions—for example, "all the stuff that circulates online"—but this too isn't quite right. Does a classic film streamed online rather than projected in a movie theater become content simply because of the context? It seems that content isn't just context specific but also subject to the eye of the beholder. I would never refer to French New Wave filmmaker Agnès Varda's vast trove of films as content, but I suspect many executives at Netflix and Amazon Prime would. In terms of classification, this makes defining content challenging. While a lot of content is produced simply to circulate as content (e.g., a blog post produced to promote a service or product), the content industry is also adept at appropriating an entire range of existing texts, images, and recordings as content. And this raises one additional question: What is the content industry?

Just as content appears to point to many different things, the content industry seems to stretch across multiple industries that may or may not hold much in common. For this reason, the content industry may be best understood as an industry that exists only in parasitical relationship to other industries, from marketing and publishing to education and entertainment.

Types of Content

To help further define content and the content industry, it is useful to consider just a few different types of content and to further consider what this classification of content fails to do.

Content Marketing

Typically, content marketing is defined as the activity of creating and sharing valuable and relevant content (or at least content that appears to be valuable and relevant). While content marketing may directly pitch a product or service, it generally aims to build an audience. For example, a life coach may start a blog to share free advice. The advice shared on the blog remains free over time, but the blog is ultimately a way for the coach to build a potential client list. At the center of content marketing is the concept of *organic growth*—a marketing strategy that compels customers to seek out businesses rather than the other way around.

Under the broader category of content marketing, several subfields exist, including branded content. Again, branded content doesn't take the form of a traditional advertisement; instead, it strives to offer information, usually in the form of a short article or video, that at least appears to be valuable and relevant. In addition, some forms of branded content seek to build brand loyalty by attaching a brand to a broader campaign. The Dove Self-Esteem Project is one example. In this case, the Dove brand created a series of advertisements and related educational resources targeting tween and teen girls that aim to send the message that girls should feel good about their bodies, whatever their size or appearance. The campaign wasn't directly selling Dove products but rather was actively working to create brand loyalty, especially among girls and their mothers, by associating Dove with a body-positive message.

Publishing Content

Although the content industry and publishing industry were once two different entities, the line between them continues to blur. While some publishers still focus on the publication of books, many—especially educational publishers—now focus on the production of content. Among other critics, Michael Bhaskar, author of *The Content Machine: Towards a Theory of Publishing from the Printing Press to the Internet* (2013), has argued that one can't separate publishing from content. As Bhaskar observes, "Wherever you find publishing, you find content."[11] While some people in the publishing industry contend that all publishing output is content, some publishers (e.g., niche literary presses) continue to talk exclusively or primarily about producing books. For the many publishers who have already embraced the idea of content, though, books are certainly no longer their exclusive focus. In the publishing industry, *content* can refer to printed books or ebooks but also to other products, such as curricular modules, online archives, and even videos. Moreover, this non-book content is not always produced to augment existing books in a publisher's catalog. As a result, the publishing industry has arguably already drifted from being an industry focused exclusively on books to one that produces other types of content, including content traditionally associated with the television and film industry.

Educational Content
Another growing and highly valuable branch of the content industry is educational content. Some educational

content overlaps with publishing content (e.g., digital content based on existing printed books). Online courses and personalized learning apps also feature educational content of varying quality. However, educational content is by no means restricted to content targeting the K–12 and higher education markets. As companies seek to streamline their training to keep existing employees up to date on new technologies and platforms, the training industry has also expanded, creating new demands for educational content targeting adult learners across sectors and over the course of the career cycle. In the twenty-first century, many private companies are educating not only their employees but also their customers and clients. For example, as artificial intelligence, machine learning, and blockchain technologies transform everything from home appliances to banking, consumers increasingly face a market dominated by products they don't yet fully understand. To help promote the sale of new and emerging products and services, private companies are increasingly also investing in the production of educational content for consumers and clients.

Entertainment Content
The most ubiquitous part of the content industry is arguably entertainment content. Entertainment content can take the form of a television series, film, video game, or

audio recording, among other forms. Most of the world's largest technology companies, from Amazon to Apple, are already engaged in the production of entertainment content. Of course, like marketing content, entertainment content often serves multiple purposes. A high percentage of the entertainment content that one encounters on platforms such as Amazon or Netflix, for example, was created first and foremost to secure subscribers. Netflix's first original production, *House of Cards*, stands as a case in point. Before *House of Cards*, Netflix was in the business of streaming productions by other studios. Beyond serving as entertainment content, *House of Cards* helped Netflix attract millions of subscribers and, in turn, fund its transformation from a streaming platform to a production studio.

In the case of entertainment content, the discussion of content gets especially confusing. From the standpoint of a large content provider such as Netflix, everything on the site may very well be categorized as content. However, some of the films available on the site were not produced as content. On sites such as Netflix, much of the "content" predates the rise of the content industry and was in circulation long before anyone was talking about content or the content industry. In this case, existing categories of film and television are, in a sense, subsumed by the broader category of content, which brings us to a final and important consideration.

The aforementioned categories certainly help to classify different types of content—for example, by distinguishing educational content from entertainment content. But what is most striking about these categories is what they fail to do: These emerging classifications don't tell us anything about genre (e.g., poetry versus fiction or sitcom versus drama), medium (e.g., print versus film), or format (e.g., 16 mm film versus video or vinyl record versus MP3). In the world of content, genre, medium, and format are secondary concerns and, in some instances, they seem to disappear entirely. We're left with a series of classifications that emphasize where or how content circulates in different sectors and markets. One might conclude that with the rise of the content industry, we have already seen a shift away from understanding cultural production in relation to aesthetic and material categories and toward understanding cultural production solely through a market-focused lens. If this is the case, the message is clear: Cultural production matters, but only to the extent that it helps drive profits in a specific market sector. What is being said, how it is being said, and via what medium are secondary to the market itself. The rise of the content industry is the ultimate expression of neoliberalism. Under the logic of neoliberalism, everything—politics, desire, sociality, art, culture, and so on—is reduced to mere nodes in the market economy. Reducing all forms of cultural production to content not only conveniently

The rise of the
content industry is
the ultimate expression
of neoliberalism.

erases the specificity of different types of cultural production but also effectively ensures that all types of cultural production can be easily substituted for each other and exchanged. After all, all content is part of a single and indistinguishable flow.

In the chapters that follow, this book delves deeper into the content industry. Subsequent chapters explore what differentiates user-generated content from content produced by compensated (albeit often grossly undercompensated) workers in content farms and how fields ranging from art and literature to journalism to politics have been affected by the rise of the content industry. Specific attention is paid to how the content industry continues to disrupt the field of cultural production, transforming it into a place where one's ability to engage in work as an artist or a writer is increasingly contingent on one's content capital; that is, on one's ability to produce content not about one's work but about one's status as an artist, writer, or performer. The book concludes by offering a preliminary look at the future of content and the content industry and the potential impact of automation, which threatens to turn content production into something increasingly divorced from human producers altogether.

USER-GENERATED CONTENT

In 2005, most writers were boycotting Amazon. At the time, the online retailer was viewed as an imminent threat to independent bookshops, though not yet as a threat to retailing as we knew it. But one writer, Kevin Killian, was secretly leaving reviews on the loathed platform. By the time of his death in 2019, Killian had published over 2,500 reviews of books, films, and miscellaneous household products on Amazon—enough reviews to earn him a spot in Amazon's "Reviewer Hall of Fame." In interviews, Killian explained that he started posting Amazon reviews after an illness left him unable to write anything of length or substance. Over time, his reviews, which were eventually compiled and published as an open-source book, would serve as more than writing therapy. In Killian's words, "I have often used Amazon reviews as a springboard to doing other kinds of writing projects. So when you read them, yeah, they're reviews of a sort, but they also seem like novels. They're poems. They're essays about life. I adopt a different persona in them. . . . So yeah, I get a lot of my kinks out there, on Amazon."[1] But Killian's Amazon reviews—a conceptual writing project that spanned more than a decade—also served another purpose. Because his reviews, which represent a type of "user-generated content," always served his own needs and not simply Amazon's, they ultimately served as an ongoing reminder of user-generated content's original promise—to collapse the line between consumers and producers.

In the 2020s, readers may have difficultly appreciating that user-generated content once appeared ripe with creative, political, and even subversive possibilities. But a time existed when optimism about user-generated content abounded. It promised to revitalize the public sphere, lay the groundwork for the rise of citizen journalism, bring marginalized voices to the center, and enable writers, musicians, filmmakers, and artists without access to publishing houses, record labels, big-time production money, or gallery or museum space to reach increasingly broad audiences. Some of these things turned out to be true. Letters to the editor are no longer the only or primary way to publicly participate in political debates as regular folks. Citizen journalism has expanded around the globe. And, for better or worse, platforms for user-generated content like Twitter, Instagram, and YouTube have created a massive audience for all sorts of rising stars, whether or not they exhibit any notable talents.

However, user-generated content—a concept that has at times been used contiguously with overlapping concepts ranging from "convergence culture" to "participatory culture" to "peer production"—wasn't just about regular people widely circulating their ideas, words, images, and performances. What most people didn't realize in the 1990s or even early 2000s is how, where, and to what ends the content they were now freely sharing online would help generate revenue for private companies and, in many cases, lay the foundation for the development of new technologies, including some that would eventually be turned against users. Concluding that the history of user-generated content is simply a history of deception would be unfair. The creators of some early user-generated platforms weren't fully aware of the potential profits they might reap from the data assets they were accumulating. Also, even well into the digital era, not all user-generated initiatives are driven by greed or big tech's desire to drive its own research and development agendas. For this reason, the history of user-generated content may be best understood as a history of conflicting desires and agendas.

The Long History of User-Generated Content

Although user-generated content may be a relatively new phenomenon, users did contribute to the creation or development of products before 2000. In fact, there is a long history of users making contributions to the production of texts and other products to which they never held copyright or ownership.

In the early years of movable type, for example, books were frequently printed dozens of times, with subsequent editions incorporating changes and corrections. In some cases, the changes and corrections were driven by the author, but other early printed books were revised and republished due to additions and revisions proposed by readers. Sebastian Munster's *Cosmography*, for example, first appeared in 1544 and went through eight editions in Munster's lifetime and another thirty-five editions by 1628. The revisions were largely the result of additions and corrections offered by his readers. In her seminal work on the history of the printing press, Elizabeth Eisenstein describes the culture of the early print world as one where editors and publishers "did not merely store data passively in compendia" but also "created vast networks of correspondents" by soliciting criticism of each edition and "sometimes publicly promising to mention the names of readers who sent in new information or who spotted the errors which would be weeded out."[2] In this respect, early printers and readers, according to Eisenstein, were engaged in endeavors that resonate with the crowd-sourced and user-generated projects that have come to define contemporary communications.

As the popularity of encyclopedias and compendiums declined, readers continued to contribute to the research and development of at least some types of texts. In 1857, the Unregistered Words Committee of the Philological Society of London issued a circular calling for volunteers to read specific books and copy out quotations that offered examples of "unregistered" words and meanings (i.e., items not yet recorded in other dictionaries). The original proposal wasn't intended to develop a complete dictionary, but as volunteers continued to respond to the Philological Society's call for assistance, a decision was made to create a new English dictionary. This user-generated experiment eventually led to the publication of the first *Oxford English Dictionary*.[3] Beyond dictionaries, user-generated content has also long been a mainstay in the travel guide industry. In the twenty-first century, TripAdvisor relies entirely on user-generated content. The platform, which was built with just $3 million in investments but was worth an estimated $7 billion by 2016, has transformed how people make decisions as they travel around the world.[4] Yet, as early as the late nineteenth century, travel guides were already being developed with the help of travelers. As John Muirhead, the English-language editor of the *Baedeker*, observed in 1889, "A guidebook is not made, it grows." Muirhead further explained, "When a new edition is being prepared, the first thing we do is to go carefully through the mass of correspondence, generally very voluminous, which has come to hand. This consists of hotel bills, notes, complaints, and suggestions."[5]

From encyclopedias to dictionaries to travel guides, there is a long history of readers contributing to the research and development of texts. But since the 1990s, three things have radically transformed how regular folks contribute to the production of texts and images of all kinds: an expanded capacity to engage in the production of audio and visual content; an expanded capacity to broadcast these creations; and most importantly, an expanded capacity for private companies to turn such creations into assets.

The Ability to Generate Content across Media

In a print culture, user-generated content was generally restricted to one type of content—text. In a digital culture, users can now share more than words. Since the launch of digital photography and mobile devices, user-generated content is now just as likely to take the form of photographs, videos, and sound recordings as it is to take the form of text. With user-generated content now being produced across media, there is more user-generated content and, more importantly, such content is no longer restricted to wordsmiths. Today, anyone, even very young children or people with limited literacy skills, can easily contribute to the content pool.

The Ability of Users to Publish/Broadcast Content

In the past, users could submit content—whether suggesting words to the editors of the *Oxford English Dictionary* or travel advice to the editors of the *Baedeker* guides—but in a print culture, such users were still entirely dependent on the editors of these volumes to put their ideas into print. In a digital era, sites may be moderated, but users can generally make a small edit to a Wikipedia page, submit a review on Yelp, or post a dance performance on YouTube without waiting for anyone's approval.

Capacity to Capture, Manage, and Profit from User-Generated Content

In the twenty-first century, user-generated content can be easily captured, managed, and transformed into an asset. To begin, user-generated content can now be captured across media twenty-four hours a day, seven days a week; and in some cases, users are not even aware that their content is being captured. Second, the ability to manage large data sets has expanded. No longer dependent on editors manually sorting through the mail, data can now be automatically collected and mined. As such, volume is no longer a concern, and this has led to another important shift.

Because we now have the capacity to capture, collect, and mine increasingly large sets of data, we can deploy user-generated content to achieve entirely different ends. Facebook's users may upload photographs in order to share memories with friends and family, but these photographs are valuable to Facebook for an entirely different reason. With millions of tagged photographs, Facebook can support the development of facial recognition technologies, among other things. Simply put, brought to scale, user-generated content exceeds its original purpose and, in the process, becomes increasingly valuable as an asset.

So, what's changed since the days of crowd-sourced encyclopedia, dictionary, and travel guide publishing? Back in the sixteenth century, if you contributed an update to Munster's *Cosmography*, your update likely remained your update—a correction or new factoid that would simply help make *Cosmography* a more accurate and relevant resource. Today, some user-generated content—for example, a correction or addition to a Wikipedia page—maintains its original purpose, but a lot of other user-generated data is collected under one pretense and then used for different purposes. User-generated content is now more likely to also circulate as, to use Lyotard's term, "investment knowledge"—knowledge exchanged to optimize the performance of an entirely separate endeavor. This may sound problematic, and in many respects it is, but this doesn't mean user-generated content has always been or currently is entirely at odds with user needs.

The Promise of User-Generated Content

To appreciate the original promise of user-generated content, consider some of the other ways in which it has been described over time. While *user-generated content* has always been the favored term in a corporate context, alternative terms such as *convergence culture*, *participatory culture*, and *peer production* have often been favored by scholars, cultural workers, and digital activists. Whether or not you opt to embrace these terms, they matter. Above all else, they remind us that before user-generated content was viewed as merely a part of the endless data stream required to fuel tech companies, it was envisioned as something that held the potential to transform culture, media, and production endeavors of all kinds.

Consider the terms *convergence culture* and *participatory culture*. Media theorist Henry Jenkins is generally credited with coining the former term and popularizing the latter. Early on, Jenkins recognized that we live in a world where content can and will be increasingly monetized by private corporations. As he observed in his 2006 book *Convergence Culture*, "corporations—and even individuals within corporate media—still exert greater power than any individual consumer or even the aggregate of consumers." Still, in retrospect, Jenkins's use of the concepts of *convergence culture* and *participatory culture* reflected a certain optimism about the world users might build online. "In a world of media convergence," Jenkins observed, "every important story gets told, every band gets sold" (cynically, he also noted that "every consumer gets courted across multiple media platforms"). He further insisted that in this new online world, "Rather than talking about media producers and consumers as occupying separate roles, we might now see them as participants who interact with each other according to a new set of rules that none of us fully understands."[6] Jenkins's position on convergence culture and participatory culture was never naïve, but it also wasn't dripping with cynicism. "Convergence culture is where old and new media collide," he concluded. It is "where grassroots and corporate media intersect, where the power of the media producer and the media consumer interact in unpredictable ways."[7] Ultimately, Jenkins imagined a world where consumers might be increasingly repositioned as producers and once-marginalized voices might finally have at least a chance of taking center stage.

Around the time that Jenkins was writing about convergence culture and participatory culture, legal scholar Yochai Benkler was sharing another vision for this new world order. Using the already-established practice of open-source software as a central example, Benkler envisioned a world where problems might be tackled with increased efficiency. In his 2002 *Yale Law Journal* article "Coase's Penguin, or, Linux and *The Nature of the Firm*," he accurately predicted that we were about to enter a "third mode of production in the digitally networked environment." Before YouTube, Facebook, or Flickr had even launched, Benkler foresaw the arrival of an era of "commons-based peer production." He used the term *peer production* to distinguish this new mode of production from earlier modes of property- and contract-based production. With peer production, Benkler observed, "groups of individuals successfully collaborate on large-scale projects following a diverse cluster of motivational drives and social signals, rather than either market prices or managerial commands."[8]

While Benkler, like Jenkins, never assumed that this emerging mode of peer production would be immune to cooptation, in 2002, his optimism seeps through. Among other things, Benkler believed that commons-based peer production would take the guesswork out of sourcing talent. After all, as he argued, "peer production has a systematic advantage over markets and firms in matching the best available human capital to the best available information inputs to create information products." That is, if in the past one had to rely on serendipity to bring together a dream team of designers or engineers to solve a problem, in the emerging commons-based peer production world, serendipity would no longer be necessary for two key reasons. First, peer production increases the chances that the best person for any given job will actually end up doing the job, because jobs that were previously closed (e.g., limited to employees with specific credentials) will be opened up to the broader public. Second, peer production removes traditional obstacles posed by property and contracts by decreasing the cost of "allowing larger clusters of potential contributors to interact with large clusters of information resources in search of new projects and opportunities for collaboration."[9] Put simply, in the world of commons-based peer production, problems are presented and solutions are crowd-sourced by the best minds around the world without all of the hassle of old-world models with their credential vetting, contracts, and expectation that collaborators will necessarily assemble in the same room and work face to face for extended periods of time.

Jenkins's and Benkler's early writings on user-generated content are by no means driven by an identical agenda, but they had at least one thing in common. Both theorists agreed that with the shift to participatory culture or peer production, more people—regardless of their identity, credentials, or locations—will be able to come together to engage in cultural production, debate issues, and solve problems. Of course, by the time Jenkins and Benkler were weighing in on this subject in scholarly publications, digital activists had been making similar arguments for well over a decade, albeit not necessarily in the form of peer-reviewed articles or university press books.

One of the earliest and most well-known groups to express the arguments later popularized by theorists such as Jenkins and Benkler was the WELL (Whole Earth 'Lectronic Link)—a freewheeling virtual community started by the same commune-supplying hippies responsible for the *Whole Earth Catalog* in the early 1970s. The WELL has always recognized that "users" (what the WELL would describe as "members") aren't just people who generate stuff to occupy virtual spaces. What members produce isn't content per se but rather a virtual form of bricks and mortar. Kevin Kelly, a cofounder of the WELL who later served as an executive editor at *Wired*, has said that when the WELL started, it was driven by seven design goals, including a commitment to making the WELL a "self-designing experiment"—that is, a place where "early users were to design the system for later users."[10] In this respect, from its inception, the WELL understood user-generated content as raw material laying the foundation for new forms of community.

Precisely because content generated by users was once viewed as both the stuff required to build new containers and the stuff that might occupy these new containers, many cyber optimists believed early on that users might eventually rebuild the world online and, in the process, overcome the entrenched inequities and access barriers of real life. On February 8, 1996, when many people were still figuring out how to connect their home modem to their desktop computer, John Perry Barlow—a cattle rancher, early member of the WELL, and founding member of the Electronic Frontier Foundation (EFF)—published his now-infamous cyber manifesto, "A Declaration of the Independence of Cyberspace." The manifesto wasn't just a call for governments around the world to back off and leave cyberspace alone. It reflected the utopian ethos prevalent at the time: the belief that users were building a new and better world online. From its opening statement— "Governments of the Industrial World . . . On behalf of the future, I ask you of the past to leave us alone. You are not welcome among us. You have no sovereignty where we gather"—to its conclusion—"We will create a civilization of the Mind in Cyberspace. May it be more humane and fair than the world your governments have made before"— Barlow meant business.[11] He wasn't alone. The manifesto and the work he would ultimately carry out through the EFF remain deeply rooted in a belief that online, users can change the world by reimagining its parameters, altering who is invited to engage in its design, and most important, by wrestling its control out of the hands of governments and handing it back to the people.

When looking back on the early days of cyberspace and writings on convergence culture, participatory culture, peer production, and the electronic frontier, one finds a lot of hope about the potential ways in which users might build new cultures, systems of exchange, and political structures. Also painfully apparent is the fact that not everyone was participating in these utopian conversations. Certainly, user-generated or participatory media may have once appeared ripe with possibilities, but most of the people writing about these possibilities (and promoting them) were still white men living in highly industrialized nations—a point that visionaries like Barlow never fully appreciated. By 2000, media theorist Lisa Nakamura could say with considerable certainty that "the Internet 'revolution' is over," and worse yet—as had already happened during most other so-called revolutions—people of color were left on the margins. As Nakamura observed at the time, even as terms such as *digital divide* started trending, people of color were functionally absent from the internet.[12] Yet, as Nakamura also contends, even with people of color occupying a marginal role online, the internet was already a place where racial identities, divides, and inequalities were being produced and reproduced.

Since Nakamura's *Cybertypes: Race, Ethnicity, and Identity on the Internet* first appeared, similar arguments have been made by other theorists about gender, ability, and geographic location. At least early on—back when a much higher percentage of online users were still building virtual infrastructure and doing so at arm's length from big tech, in alternative communities like the WELL—users may have been dreaming big, but those users certainly didn't represent everyone who could have been participating in this world-building endeavor. To be clear, virtual communities would eventually become far more diverse. The Pew Research Center found that in 2000, 38 percent of Black Americans reported using the internet compared to 53 percent of white Americans. By 2018, the gap had closed.[13] What changed during that time is important. In 2000, more spaces online were still transaction-free, and a higher percentage of users were still actively engaged in building online communities from the ground up rather than simply adding content to sites and platforms owned by outside entities. As access expanded, virtual communities became increasingly diverse, but unfortunately this expansion coincided with the decline of most early utopian virtual communities and the rise of transactional communities (e.g., those supported by established social media platforms).

When User-Generated Content Became an Asset

In the mid-1990s, many people were optimistic about the potential ways that users might rebuild the world online, but they weren't all cyber enthusiasts. By that time, user-generated content was also attracting attention from another demographic—big business. With digital business still in a nascent stage, business analysts were even actively looking at underground communities, including the WELL, to figure out how to start profiting from the world's growing digital outputs.

In "Real Profits from Virtual Communities," an article published in a 1995 issue of the *McKinsey Quarterly*, a team of McKinsey & Company analysts observed, "Electronic communities have actually existed for many years. Groups like The Well have spawned strong relationships and developed their own norms and sense of history." The authors of the article recognized that these communities are "noncommercial"—that is, "Communication, entertainment, and information are their reasons for being, and contracts tend to be in barter form. Financial transactions are rare, and often resisted." Still, they were also confident that "new kinds of community that are more commercially focused will emerge soon."[14]

The consultants at McKinsey were right. Shortly after the publication of "Real Profits from Virtual Communities," online communities started to become increasingly transactional. As the McKinsey analysts predicted, while some online community members did remain resistant to turning their communities into transactional environments (to this day, the WELL is still a nonprofit endeavor), as more people went online, consumers—rather than visionaries—increasingly started to shape the online world. But this isn't the only thing McKinsey's analysts accurately predicted in 1995. They also foresaw the potential for virtual communities to become valuable assets in a unique new way. Without entirely discounting the possibility that profits might still be derived from eventually making virtual communities subscription-based, they predicted that the real profits would ultimately come from the "unique content" virtual community members would generate. The shift from old-world approaches to profit (i.e., subscriptions) to new-world approaches (i.e., turning user-generated content into an asset that can be collected, mined, and sold) wouldn't be simple. Among other challenges, McKinsey's analysts cautioned, "Aspiring community organizers will have to decide which communities they will try to own. Their decision will be based partly on the assets that they already possess, such as brands, content, special skills, and relationships with other communities."[15] Many other questions remained unanswered in 1995: How will we structure ownership of user-generated content? Must these virtual communities be heavily moderated to ensure only the right type of content is generated by users? Who will be charged with the moderation of these communities? What types of skills will these moderators need and where will they receive their training? Yet what was clear as early as 1995 was the potential to turn virtual communities—their participants, infrastructure, and especially their unique content—into assets.

In retrospect, what is most interesting about this period of internet history is the notable disconnect between what business analysts and businesses were plotting and what most online users understood about these future plans. After all, in the 1990s and even well into the early 2000s, while business analysts and businesses were actively exploring how to turn users' comments and, eventually, users' digital photographs, videos, and sound files into assets, most online users remained largely in the dark about the ways in which their digital output might be monetized. This is not to suggest that early online users were completely oblivious. Most people anticipated that the internet would become more commercialized. In the 1990s, many people were already worrying that free sites might eventually be accessible only with a paid subscription and that websites would eventually be cluttered with advertisements and, as a result, start to look a lot more like the average newspaper or magazine. What most people wandering through the "electronic frontier" for the first time didn't realize in 1995 or even 2000 was that the comments they were freely sharing online were already being viewed as a potential asset by a new class of entrepreneurs. This lack of awareness is presumably why few users were concerned about freely sharing information, even private information, on social media platforms such as Facebook and photo- and video-sharing sites such as YouTube and Flickr when they began to appear in the early

2000s. While a real concern existed that these newfangled forms of entertainment and communication might eventually require a high subscription fee or be colonized by advertisements, few people were worrying that these sites might eventually transform everything—even conversations with friends or exchanges of personal photographs of birthdays and bat mitzvahs—into assets. But this is precisely what happened: private companies learned to exploit users' online interactions and creativity (i.e., their content).

As Christian Fuchs argued in his 2013 essay "Class and Exploitation on the Internet," user-generated data is best understood as a commodity that is partially produced by users and partially produced by the corporations that build and maintain the platforms adopted by users. However, as Fuchs further commented, one notable difference exists between these two players—"users are unpaid and therefore infinitely exploited."[16] Being unpaid doesn't mean that these users aren't, as scholars such as Jenkins have long emphasized, also active participants. As Fuchs suggests, "On Facebook, Twitter, and blogs, users are fairly active and creative . . . but this active character is the very source of exploitation."[17] Ultimately, the ability of private companies to exploit users' online interactions and creativity (i.e., their content) would drive the success of the digital economy.

Ultimately, the ability of private companies to exploit users' online interactions and creativity (i.e., their content) would drive the success of the digital economy.

The Classification of User-Generated Content

Three decades after the arrival of the web, user-generated content has become ubiquitous. In the process, it has transformed nearly every sector imaginable from entertainment and education to health and finance. User-generated content has also restructured our everyday practices—it has altered how and what we cook, how we learn, where we travel, and even who we date. Still, disagreements about user-generated content abound. Optimists argue that such content has brought new efficiencies into our lives (e.g., user-generated content can be collected and mined to strengthen the supply chain and ensure the right volume of products are available in the right place at the right time). Pessimists say that user-generated content has eroded our privacy and, worse yet, turned us all into digital laborers who are expected to toil away—without compensation—twenty-four hours a day. Despite the fact that user-generated content—love it or loathe it—has transformed and continues to transform how we work, play, and live, the classification of user-generated content remains a challenge.

On Wikipedia, which is just one example of user-generated content, the entry on "user-generated content" (at least the entry that existed when I wrote this chapter) lists eight "types" of user-generated content: blogs, websites, video games, advertising, retailers, educational, photo sharing, and short video sharing. What's striking about the entry is that the types of user-generated content listed don't appear to reflect any classificatory logic at all. A blog is arguably a specific genre of online writing; a website is a collection of web pages; a video game is a type of game; and advertising, photo sharing, and video sharing are all practices that can take place either online or off. Simply put, the Wiki entry attempts but fails to classify different types of user-generated content because it endeavors to compare genres to collections to practices. Listing blogs, websites, and video games under the same broad category is a bit like listing novels, archives, and games in the same category. As a classification, it doesn't make much sense. Yet, once one starts to contemplate how to update the Wiki entry on user-generated content, classifying such content becomes far more challenging.

To begin, one might approach the update by classifying user-generated content in relation to established media categories (e.g., text, image, sound). At the very least, this approach would reveal how user-generated content operates across media. But since all digital user-generated content is streamable, old-world divisions between text, image, and sound ultimately reveal little about the differences between different types of user-generated content. Said another way, while the differences between a book, a printed photograph, and a vinyl record may be significant, the differences between a blog post, a digital photograph, and an MP3 are less clear. So, what if one focused instead on the function of different types of user-generated content?

Classifying user-generated content by function might draw attention to content whose primary function is to review products or services (comments left on a platforms like Yelp or Amazon); share opinions (reader comments on the *New York Times* or Fox News site); entertain (videos on YouTube or Vimeo); offer feedback on the user's health, habits, or lifestyle (Fitbit); connect with family and friends (Facebook or Instagram); and so on. This classification might be helpful, but it would remain entirely user-centric, and as previously noted, user-generated content is often employed in ways entirely unknown to the people who generated the content. A more difficult but by no means less important endeavor, then, would be to classify user-generated content in relation to how it is used by the owners of digital platforms that rely on user-generated content. Such a classification system might separate user-generated content produced for the pharmaceutical industry (the user-generated data about monthly periods left on Clue) from user-generated content produced to drive facial recognition technologies (photographs posted on Facebook and Instagram). But again, this classification would still fail to capture the fact that the content in question isn't just generated or used for one purpose or by one entity. The user-generated content shared by users on the family-history site Ancestry.com, which includes genetic data, not only supports the platform's own research and development (helping the company to improve its platform) but also is used to support research in other fields, including the pharmaceutical industry.

As data is posted, collected, combined, mined, and traded, both its original medium and message cease to matter. As such, any attempt to classify user-generated content based on medium or message is bound to run into problems. Rather than attempting to classify types of user-generated content, it may be more valuable to focus on tracing its life cycle. Ultimately, what distinguishes digital user-generated content from early forms of user-generated content and other types of digital content (e.g., content produced by the owners of platforms) is its capacity to morph over time—to transform from a communicative act originating from a single user to one small bit of data in a larger database, and then to a form of investment knowledge that exists to optimize services, products, and schemes that the original user may have never imagined possible.

CONTENT FARMS

If you know where to look, you can find writing turned out by professionals and edited to meet industry standards just about anywhere. But for every reputable article circulating online, thousands of others range from just okay to downright bad.

In the "okay" category, there are millions of articles composed of actual sentences with a low enough ratio of grammatical errors to make them more or less readable. These include articles that are generally correct but not particularly compelling, such as "How to Hang a Decorative Tray" on eHow. In addition to all the okay writing in circulation, a lot of writing is downright bad. Consider, for example, the following statement published on a popular astrology site: "You need to work hard for improving the opportunities for gaining finance." Sadly, this example is not an exception to the rule. Most people who spend any time online spend much of it skimming texts composed of material just like the material cited here. But where does all this bad writing—commonly known as clickbait—originate? To answer this question, turn back the clock to a time when "google" had not yet become widely adopted as a verb and the content industry was still in its infancy.

Writing in the Age of Digital *Incunabula*

Incunabula, a Latin term that literally means "in the cradle," is generally used to describe the small cache of books that was produced during the first few decades of print culture in the late fifteenth century, or what historians describe as the "Age of Incunabula." In the history of print culture, the *incunabula* era is significant because it marked a brief interval when old and new methods of book production—those associated with the scriptoriums of the Middle Ages and those associated with the emerging technology of movable type—overlapped. Not unlike the overlap between scribal and print cultures in the late fifteenth century, for a brief period—perhaps only a decade—efforts to experiment with new and emerging digital technologies remained profoundly shaped by our print-centric expectations. For example, many early visitors to the web not only expected to encounter grammatically correct sentences with standardized spelling but also familiar formatting conventions. As a result, early websites often featured hangovers from print culture. In 1995 or 1996, it wasn't unusual to find website creators still underlining book titles and indenting paragraphs, just as they would have done on a typewriter back in the 1980s.

In the 1990s, the written word did begin to change, but initially, the impact of the internet on writing was surprisingly slow. In fact, if people were concerned about the future of writing in the 1990s, fear of the unknown was as much a factor as the hard evidence that the written word was suddenly undergoing a catastrophic shift. This concern largely reflects the fact that in the 1990s the web was still a black hole understood by few and feared by many more.

A 1995 article in the *New York Times* compared the web to "a Bermuda Triangle in the information ocean" and more scathingly, to "the junk food aisle in cyberspace's digital supermarket."[1] Two years later, the author of an article published in the *Chronicle of Higher Education* suggested, "Search engines, with their half-baked algorithms, are closer to slot machines than library catalogues. You throw your query to the wind, and who knows what will come back to you?"[2] The coauthors of an article in *Tech-Trends* chose a more whimsical analogy to help readers understand the web: "The World Wide Web is like an open flea market. Anyone can come in and display whatever they choose and people visiting can select items they want to examine and keep."[3] Perhaps most surprising, however, is that even early internet enthusiasts often adopted analogies that appeared intent on highlighting the web's unknowable or uncontainable nature. In the introduction to his 1993 book *The Virtual Community*, digital evangelist Howard Rheingold, who had helped found the WELL—one of the world's first virtual communities—compared the web to "a bacterial colony."[4]

From the danger of a black hole and the chance operations of a slot machine to the randomness of a flea market and the uncontainable growth of a bacterial colony, during the age of digital *incunabula*, the web was largely unknown, misunderstood, and to some people, frightening. Whatever the web was, even early on, it was a place where a lot of bad writing was already accumulating. What many people born in the late 1990s or beyond don't appreciate is that the early web didn't look at all like the current web with its social media sites, image-sharing platforms, and video- and sound-streaming capabilities. For most of the 1990s, this apparently chaotic, uncontainable, and even frightening space was almost exclusively composed of texts, so reading and writing rather than listening or viewing were the default. As a result, concerns about the web's impact on writing were never far from the surface. What few people predicted in the 1990s was that the worst was still to come.

Domain Building and the Birth of Clickbait

By the early 2000s, e-commerce was already well established. While we may have been a long way from the on-demand shopping culture that has since become ubiquitous, by that period the idea of using a credit card to make an online purchase was at least becoming mainstream. Around this time a new generation of web entrepreneurs appeared. Unlike an earlier generation of web entrepreneurs who had either a product or a service to sell, these new entrepreneurs didn't have much to sell at all. Instead, they were going online because they had discovered that they could make a lot of money without selling or doing anything—that is, if they had a website where they could run online advertisements. This period is also when the web started to have a profound impact not only on why a lot of writing was being produced but also on the nature of this writing and the conditions of its production.

To be clear, the web was never entirely free of advertisements, but until the early 2000s, the ability to sell advertising space was mostly limited to people running legitimate businesses. If you've ever wondered who is to blame for introducing advertisements to the web, a good place to start is with Hotwired—a commercial web magazine launched by Wired Ventures (the same entity that originally owned the digital culture magazine *Wired*). Hotwired was the first company to sell what are generally known as banner ads. The banner ad model wasn't very innovative; it was essentially a digital version of old-style print-based advertising. People with something to sell would purchase space—in this case, a portion of a website and usually a high-profile "banner" at the top of the page—and pay upfront to occupy this online real estate for a set amount of time.[5] Of course, unless you had a lot of money to pay for upfront advertising space or you had the resources and staff to go out and attract potential advertisers, you likely weren't buying or selling online advertisements in the 1990s. Then, Google, and eventually everyone else, entered a new era of advertising, which ultimately would prove to have the greatest impact on writing in the digital era.

AdWords and AdSense are two of Google's many "vertical products," meaning they are both products connected to Google's search function that do something else—in this case, help people buy advertisements or turn their websites into advertising venues. AdWords appeared first in 2000 and was based on a simple premise. Let's say you own a solarium building company, and you want anyone who searches the terms "solarium construction" or "solarium contractor" to find your business's homepage. If you purchase these keywords from Google (a simple task if you have a credit card), anyone searching these terms will now be presented with the terms and a link to your website. While advertisers now bid on keywords (paying more for more popular search terms), when AdWords first launched in 2000, paid searches were a bargain. To occupy the top spot in any search, advertisers paid just $15 per 1,000 exposures or views.[6] What AdWords didn't do was help the average person turn his or her own website into a potential advertising space—this happened three years later with the arrival of AdSense.[7]

With AdSense, anyone who owned a domain and had a website with a bit of content could now sign up and start automatically running advertisements on their site. And just like AdWords, Google made the process extraordinarily simple. Since AdSense launched in 2003, the process has more or less involved just four simple steps. First, you need to own a domain and have a website. This first step has always been easy and accessible to the masses because most domains were relatively inexpensive (on average, you can still purchase one for just a few dollars per year); also, as of AdSense's launch in 2003, you haven't needed to know anything about HTML to build a decent-looking website. Second, you have to have some content on your site. While guidelines about what type of content is acceptable have changed over time, Google has never let domain owners throw up advertisements on an empty site. Third, you have to apply for an AdSense account, but this is also a relatively simple process and, again, the application costs nothing. Once approved, Google gives you access to a tiny bit of code that you copy and paste onto your website.

This may sound confusing, but anyone who has ever used a WordPress site and knows how to locate the copy-and-paste function on their keyboard can likely figure out how and where to insert this code (and if you're confused, thousands of DIY websites and YouTube videos can walk you through the steps). Then, next thing you know, without ever having approached an advertiser, anyone—including people who may not know much at all about how to build a website or how to buy or sell advertisements or even how to run a business—can display advertisements on a personal domain and, before long, start collecting advertising revenues from Google.

As one might imagine, AdSense struck a chord with a lot of people. Suddenly, all sorts of people who had established domains to share information about their hobby—for example, fly fishing, crocheting, or antique clock restoration—were running advertisements on their personal domains and getting monthly checks from Google. Unfortunately, most money earned on AdSense turned out to be small amounts because Google gives domain owners only a portion of all advertising revenues. In fact, domain owners make just a few cents for every impression (an impression takes place when someone lands on a site with an AdSense advertisement), and a few more cents if a visitor actually clicks on an advertisement.

To make real money on AdSense—not $50 a month but $5,000 or $50,000 a month—one had to learn how to

To make real money on AdSense—not $50 a month but $5,000 or $50,000 a month—one had to learn how to play the AdSense game and play it well.

play the AdSense game and play it well. First, if a domain owner was really serious, he or she needed a lot of pages. On AdSense, eight or eighty pages might generate enough revenue to buy a nice bottle of wine at the end of the month, but it has never been enough to quit your day job. To do that, domain owners have always needed hundreds of pages. Even then, one's site or sites would have to be extremely popular, attracting tens of thousands of visitors each day. Second, domain owners needed content capable of attracting many visitors and keeping them on a site long enough to view and, most importantly, click on multiple advertisements. Finally, this new breed of web entrepreneur needed what Google has come to describe over time, albeit somewhat vaguely, as "unique and relevant" content. While initially one could get away with throwing almost anything up on a website and still reasonably expect to get AdSense approval, by 2011, Google's search algorithm had been modified to weed out so-called violators—websites populated with spam, unoriginal content, and content crammed with keywords designed to push the site to the top of any search. On the surface, Google's demand for unique and relevant content was a good thing—after all, who doesn't want to weed out online crap? But ultimately, Google's increased insistence on unique and relevant content would also set the stage for what happened next—the rise of a genre that is now known as clickbait and the rapid expansion of content farms.

What continues to deceive many readers is that clickbait is really just a frame for advertisements, even if it appears to be the main show.

Unlike the content one encounters in most books, newspapers, or magazines, clickbait's primary aim has never been to convey information or tell a story. As a result, the content found on many websites isn't the center—in essence, it is just a place where one can display AdSense advertisements. What continues to deceive many readers is that clickbait—and this includes all of those articles readers stumble across on familiar sites like eHow, Tripsavvy, Investopedia, and many others—is really just a frame for advertisements, even if it appears to be the main show.

For example, a reader might think she has stumbled across a site with fantastic information about how to become a teacher or an engineer. In fact, most career sites were made with an entirely different purpose in mind—namely, to create a space in which to place AdSense advertisements and generate revenue for the domain owner. This doesn't necessarily mean the content is always bad—sometimes it is good enough—but the error is assuming that the content was generated with the purpose of sharing information about becoming a teacher or an engineer or anything else. The thing about careers is that everyone needs one or has one but wants a new one, and so career websites are generally popular and age well over time; as a result, they are easy to monetize. The same holds true for many health-related sites. We all have aches and pains, and most people can't resist searching their symptoms online, so health-related sites such as WebMD, which was started by a web entrepreneur, not a healthcare professional, are also popular. The growing need for content that meets Google's "unique and relevant" criteria, however, would also eventually lead to the rapid growth of the content farm industry.

Life Down on the Content Farms

For a website to hold readers long enough to generate a reasonable number of impressions and clicks, it needs to be *search-engine-optimized*—that is, written with the sole purpose of ranking first in any search. As a rule of thumb, each page should contain at least 300 words, though longer (600 to 1,000 words) is generally considered better. A 300-page site, then, generally requires at least 100,000 words, which is about three times the length of the book you're currently reading. Long before clickbait existed, the best print magazines were paying a dollar a word. A mediocre print publication might have paid closer to thirty cents per word, but even at that rate, writers could expect to take home about $100 to $150 for a short article. From the beginning, these rates were never offered to writers turning out most online content.

In 2009, *Wired* published the first of what would be many articles on the emerging world of content farms. In one of these early articles, Daniel Roth investigated Demand Media. Demand Media, now known as Leaf Group, owns a number of familiar content sites including eHow and TechWalla. When Roth carried out his investigation in 2009, he found an emerging industry where white-collar labor—the sort of work done by writers and editors—was already grossly undervalued. "It's the online equivalent of day laborers waiting in front of Home Depot," explained Roth. "Writers can typically select 10 articles at a time; videographers can hoard 40. Nearly every freelancer scrambles to load their assignment queue with titles they can produce quickly and with the least amount of effort—because pay for individual stories is so lousy, only a high-speed, high-volume approach will work. The average writer earns $15 per article for pieces that top out at a few hundred words, and the average filmmaker about $20 per clip, paid weekly via PayPal."[8] While this process may sound problematic—and it is—at the time, Demand Media's goal was to produce 1 million pieces of content each month (by comparison, in 2009, the *New York Times* was turning out only about 5,000 articles a month). The only way Demand could achieve its goal and guarantee a strong return was to keep its overhead, especially its labor costs, as low as possible, and as Roth discovered, they were successfully doing just that.

Despite Google's efforts to clamp down on content farms over the years, not much has changed since Roth exposed the dismal labor conditions at Demand Media in 2009. Clickbait still dominates the web. While writing this chapter, I logged on to the online work platform Upwork to survey the current going rates for content producers. The day I logged on to the platform, someone had just posted a writing job that didn't pay at all. In this case, the job poster was looking for a 1,000-word article on firearms. Any writer who produced an article that met the job poster's guidelines (which would be provided only after the so-called hire was approved) was being promised a five-star rating on Upwork (notably, employers rate freelancers on Upwork, but freelancers are never permitted to rate employers) and the potential of long-term work. The potential long-term work was also poorly compensated. In this case, the writer who ultimately won the job would be awarded "an ongoing writing gig" that entailed producing two articles a week at two cents per word. Since the articles needed to range from 1,000 to 2,500 words each, the ultimate reward was an opportunity to turn out 2,000 to 5,000 words per week for anywhere from $40 to $100. Finally, as is true of most content writing gigs, the writer would be required to relinquish copyright privileges and credit for the work since it would be posted under a pseudonym. Sadly, however exploitative this gig may be, in the content farm world, it isn't as bad as it gets.

The same afternoon I discovered this posting on Upwork, I found many others that were even more exploitative.

One recruiter wanted "peoples [sic] to write many descriptions for a virtual product." In this case, the poster was so desperate to get the product descriptions that he or she was even incentivizing the process by offering $3 for a 300-word "unique quality description" but $4 if delivered in twenty-four hours, $5 if delivered in twelve hours, and $6 if delivered in three hours or less. If $3 for 300 words isn't already bad enough, another recruiter was offering to pay a mere $3 for a 1,000-word article (less than one cent a word). Perhaps recognizing that the rate was ridiculously low, the recruiter noted that one didn't need to be a native English speaker to apply, but also warned applicants, "We don't allow article spinning, sentence restructuring and plagiarism. If you do any of these, I will report it to Upwork."[9]

These posts raise an obvious question: Who is crazy and desperate enough to write under these conditions, and why do they do it?

Factors that Contributed to the Rise of Content Farms

One might assume that most people who end up working in the content industry have little or no formal training in journalism nor any background in writing or literature. While this may account for some of the people who find themselves working in the very lowest-end content farm gigs, don't assume that everyone turning out clickbait is necessarily someone who knows nothing about writing or just doesn't care. To understand why a surprising number of people producing crappy online writing know more about writing than one might suspect, it's important to consider two relatively recent shifts that have profoundly impacted labor markets and hiring practices in North America and around the world.

The Gig Economy and Work Platforms

During the early 2000s, a new generation of web platforms appeared that were designed to help people looking for work find people who needed something done and were willing to pay for it, and vice versa. While some online work platforms have a specific focus (e.g., Uber helps people looking for rides find drivers), other online work platforms cast the net much wider. On Elance, which originally launched in 1999 and eventually merged with oDesk to form Upwork in 2015, one could hire someone to edit a book or produce content for their website or build a website from scratch or edit a series of podcasts. At first, the arrival of sites like Elance were a welcome development for freelancers. With online work platforms, finding clients outside one's own locale became easier; although Elance did pocket a small fee each time a freelancer billed a client, the onus was no longer on freelancers to track down clients who refused to pay. For people looking to hire a writer, editor, web developer, or designer, Elance also simplified finding qualified people to get a job done whatever one's timeframe or budget. These platforms played a critical part in the rise of the so-called gig economy.

Gig economy optimists—people like economist Richard Florida—argue that with the rise of the gig economy, we are finally all free to work wherever and whenever we like. On the surface, this newfound flexibility is a good thing. Theoretically, a more flexible work schedule should lead to a better work-life balance and greater engagement at work.[10] But what some people continue to celebrate as the rise of creative labor—the ability to get paid to do work we love, anytime and anywhere—others view as a mass deskilling of labor that was once valued. British cultural critic Angela McRobbie warns that by embracing gig work in what Florida dubs the "creative economy," we may be able to set our own schedules and get paid to do what we love (e.g., writing, designing clothes, or producing films), but we also give up a lot in the process. Most notably, entering the gig economy, we give up many of the things that educated, middle-class people once took for granted. This includes the reasonable expectation of access to steady employment, benefits, and the prospect of eventually retiring with at least some financial peace of mind.[11]

Whatever your political position on online work platforms and the gig economy, these connected technological and economic shifts appear to have played a role in the rise of the content farm industry. If you want to hire ten writers, you might be able to do so locally, but if you need to hire hundreds or even thousands of writers, you'll need access to a much larger qualified labor pool. Fortunately, the latter is no longer likely to pose much of a problem for two reasons. First, as already noted, work platforms facilitate such mass-scale hiring. Second, as platforms like Elance and eventually Upwork appeared, something else happened—the number of highly literate but underemployed and undercompensated university graduates increased. No one can say for certain how many humanities graduates have worked or do work for content farms (to date, I have found no studies on this subject). But anecdotally, humanities graduates, including those who fall into the underemployed or undercompensated category, appear to be well represented in the content farm sector.[12] If this is true, it may simply reflect the fact that since the 1970s, universities have been turning out more graduates in the humanities fields and that the percentage of humanities graduates finding work in relevant fields upon graduation has declined.[13] Still, the arrival of work platforms and an increasingly desperate yet highly literate workforce isn't the only factor that has arguably supported the success of content farms since 2000.

Rise of the Global Workforce
The second factor supporting the rise of the content farm industry over the past two decades is the expansion of the

global workforce. Some industries, especially manufacturing, have been exploiting global labor for centuries, but with the rise of online work platforms, exploiting people beyond one's local region got a lot easier. A small business owner in Southern California, for example, who needs a website designed or some content for his or her website can opt to hire local labor, but if they don't want to pay US rates, they now have another option. Rather than hire a US-based designer or writer or even one based in another English-language nation, the small business owner can now easily hire someone based in an emerging economy (perhaps an English-educated professional based in Karachi or Nairobi) who might be willing to do the same job for a fraction of the price. A study by the Oxford Internet Institute, based on data from four popular online labor sites (Fiverr, Freelancer, Guru, and PeoplePerHour), found that half of the top twenty nations for online labor are former British colonies, with India, Pakistan, and Bangladesh occupying the top spots.

Professionals working in emerging economies are certainly not to blame for the low rates of compensation found on platforms like Fiverr, Freelancer, or Upwork, but their presence does change the rules of the game by encouraging US-based employers and those based in other established economies to see just how far their hiring dollars can go in the online global labor market.

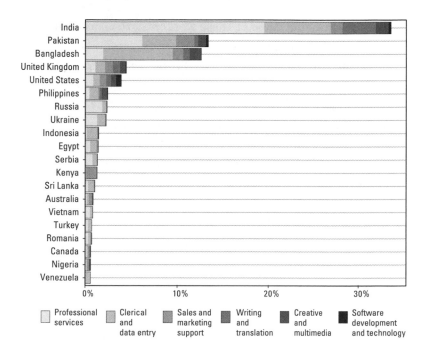

Figure 2 Online Labour Index top twenty worker home countries, July 1–6, 2017. Credit: The iLabour Project, Oxford Internet Institute.

This chapter opened with a question that most people who have spent any time online have asked at some point: Where does all that bad writing—commonly known as clickbait—originate? The answer is simple. Most crappy writing found online is produced by remote workers connected to content farms or online work platforms. But you can't assume that none of these workers care about writing. In fact, as argued, a series of recent economic shifts has created a surplus of writers, editors, researchers, and designers who are either underemployed or simply undercompensated and searching for side gigs. Content farms and online work platforms have conveniently exploited this demographic. But content farms and work platforms are responsible for even more than the millions of pages of branded content and content that exists only to generate revenue from AdSense placements. As discussed in chapter 5, since 2010 content farms and work platforms have also been implicated in the spread of "fake news," which continues to do a lot more harm than any sloppily composed sentence ever will.

CONTENT CAPITAL

In April 2014, Amalia Ulman—at the time, a recent art
school graduate living in Los Angeles—started to upload
images of herself to Instagram. Her first image, accompa-
nied by the caption "Excellences & Perfections," received
twenty-eight likes. Over the coming months, Ulman continued to upload selfies documenting her semifictional-
ized makeover. Some of the images, like the one in which
she pretended to be recovering from breast augmentation
surgery, were pure fiction. Others, including those taken
at her pole-dancing lessons, reflected things she was actually doing as part of her self-transformation. Like millions of other young women who post selfies on Instagram
every day, Ulman was using the platform to construct a
semifictional narrative about herself. Unlike most young
women, however, her carefully curated postings about
her life would ultimately be embraced as art. As art critic

Erik Morse explains in a 2015 article on Ulman's work, "promises of voyeuristic spectacle and salacious confession ignited her account's real-time fan base and drew mainstream coverage from pop culture glossies like *New York Magazine, i-D* and *Dazed and Confused*." But according to Morse, Ulman didn't just garner an online following during her durational performance on Instagram. "What continues to fascinate most about Ulman's progressing oeuvre," Morse observes, "is not only the vast conceptual net under which she interrogates theories of identity, domesticity and fantasy, but the challenging heterogeneity of disciplines and templates that she engages from exhibition to exhibition—from poetry to design to online performance."[1]

The critical reception of Ulman's social media performance work hasn't always been as positive as Morse's laudatory review, but it has been copious, and in a content age, quantity is what matters. After all, many reviews and mentions—even negative—generally do more to promote a writer's or artist's work than a single obscure review, no matter how positive that review may be.

But whether one agrees that Ulman is a social-media-era Sophie Calle or just a young woman trying to turn her selfies into art may be beside the point. For the purposes of this discussion, what is most notable are Ulman's reasons for launching the performance that would eventually come be known as *Excellences & Perfections* and what these motivations reveal about the current field of cultural production. As Ulman explained in a 2018 statement in *Artforum*, "There is an expectation now that artists should be online and on social media promoting themselves, but that the promotion shouldn't be the work per se. It felt like a requirement, especially as a woman, to expose oneself to sell the work in a way."[2]

Ulman's decision to produce content about herself (not herself as an artist but simply as a young, sexualized woman) ultimately proved wildly successful—more successful than her previous artwork. What Ulman's online

Figure 3 Amalia Ulman, *Excellences & Perfections* (screen shot of Amalia Ulman's Instagram page, November 28, 2020).

performance revealed is that in an age of content, content isn't just something that is needed to promote your art. Increasingly, content *is* art or, at least, what has come to stand in for art. The question that remains is, What does this mean for cultural producers and, more broadly, the field of cultural production? If they must produce content—not necessarily about their writing or art but about themselves—in order to thrive as writers or artists, is culture itself now nothing more or less than the sum of the content they generate about the alleged life of the author or artist?

The Field of Cultural Production before Content

In his essay "The Field of Cultural Production," French sociologist Pierre Bourdieu describes the field where cultural production (i.e., the production of literature, art, music, and so on) takes place as a "site of struggles." Using literature as a central example, Bourdieu observes that in the field of cultural production, "What is at stake is the power to impose the dominant definition of the writer and therefore to delimit the population of those entitled to take part in the struggle to define the writer." He further observes:

> In short, the fundamental stake in literary struggles is the monopoly of literary legitimacy, i.e., *inter alia*,

the monopoly of the power to say with authority who are authorized to call themselves writers; or, to put it another way, it is the monopoly of the power to consecrate producers or products (we are dealing with a world of belief and the consecrated writer is the one who has the power to consecrate and to win assent when he or she consecrates an author or a work—with a preface, a favourable review, a prize, etc.).[3]

Bourdieu recognized that a similar situation holds true for artists, musicians, and so on. On this basis, building on the work of literary critic Lucien Goldmann, Bourdieu concludes, "Understanding a work of art . . . is a matter of understanding the social group from which and for which the artist composes his work, and which, at once patron and addressee, efficient cause and final cause, creates with and, as it were, through him."[4]

Bourdieu's work on the field of cultural production highlights that writers and artists, like literature and art, are the result of a series of "position-takings" that effectively determine what counts as literature, what counts as art, and who can claim those venerated but not necessarily lucrative positions known as "author" or "artist." Bourdieu not only describes the field or site of struggles in which literature and art and its makers are produced, however, but also observes that this field is profoundly shaped by various forms of capital—not just economic capital but also cultural and symbolic capital. Of specific concern, for Bourdieu, is the idea of *cultural capital*.

According to Bourdieu, one's cultural capital—that is, one's competencies, skills, and qualifications (this includes one's knowledge of and firsthand experiences of literature, art, philosophy and so on)—enables one to more easily engage in the position-takings that structure the field of cultural production. Consider, for example, how an entirely white painting in a gallery setting might be viewed by someone with the competencies, skills, and qualifications acquired over the course of a typical liberal arts education compared to how it might be viewed by someone who never completed a liberal arts degree, never attended college, or never spent time exploring art in galleries and museums. The former individual may not like all-white paintings, but likely has the cultural capital needed to recognize such objects as art and to even appreciate them as a metacritique of art. Someone with less cultural capital may not recognize a white painting as art at all and would likely not appreciate how an entirely white canvas may even operate as a statement about art itself. The art object in question is the same; cultural capital is what largely determines whether or not the object will be recognized as art and appreciated on any level. In a content age, the entire nature of such position-takings has shifted. To appreciate the nature of this shift, returning to Ulman's work is useful.

The field of cultural production in which Ulman operates is certainly still a site of struggles, as Bourdieu suggests, and it is still partially structured by traditional forms of reception and circulation. The reviews of her work in publications such as *Art Review*, the exhibition of her work at the Tate Modern in London and the New Museum in New York City, and the broader discussion of the work beyond the art world (e.g., in fashion magazines such as *Elle*) have all contributed to her success as an artist. But in Ulman's case, something else is at work. Her successful position-takings in the modern art world first and foremost had to do with her willingness to produce content about her life and share it on a social media platform. And Ulman isn't alone. Countless young artists, writers, and musicians also increasingly rely on tactics not unlike Ulman's to secure success in a cultural field. In this respect, while the field of cultural production still exists, position-takings increasingly pivot around a writer's or an artist's ability to successfully acquire and deploy an entirely new form of capital—*content capital*.

Content Capital

Content capital is not unlike other forms of capital to the extent that it influences one's ability to engage in position-takings within a field, such as cultural production. Not unlike cultural capital, for example, it is a type of largely intangible asset that influences one's social mobility. But this may be where the similarities between content capital and other types of capital (cultural, symbolic, or economic) begin and end. Unlike cultural capital, which people acquire only through their education, travel, and access to culture and cultural institutions or venues (e.g., galleries, museums, orchestral performances, etc.), content capital is more easily acquired. You can, after all, acquire a great deal of content capital without paying for an expensive education at a private boarding school, purchasing season tickets to the opera, or spending thousands of dollars on plane tickets to visit foreign locations around the world. One builds up one's content capital simply by hanging out online and, more precisely, by posting content that garners a response and, in turn, leads to more followers and more content. While economic capital isn't always required to acquire cultural capital, it generally helps. But in the case of content capital, lack of economic capital isn't a barrier. After all, you don't have to pay to get on a platform to start generating and sharing content.

To appreciate how content capital works, consider the very different experiences that a fourteen-year-old girl living with her working-class parents in a small town in the US Midwest might have in attempting to acquire cultural versus content capital. Restricted by her location (a rural area in the Midwest) and economic condition (working class), the teenager would most likely struggle to gain access to cultural capital. The teenager in question wouldn't be able to easily attend an art opening or a live opera or orchestral performance, enroll in conservatory music lessons, study Latin, or experience foreign travel. In fact, she may not even realize that doing such things could be a gateway to acquiring the cultural capital needed to, let's say, increase her chances of gaining a spot at Yale or Harvard and, more importantly, fitting in socially and succeeding at such institutions. In the age of content, however, the same teenager, despite her limited cultural and economic resources, can acquire considerable content capital—that is, assuming she has access to three things: a digital device, a stable Wi-Fi connection, and time (ideally lots of it). Given that these are things most adolescents growing up in developed countries do have, even for individuals from modest backgrounds, content capital is arguably available for the taking.

An extreme but not rare example can be found in the surprising breakthroughs made by teen social media influencers. Some twenty-first-century teen influencers hail from small towns and modest backgrounds and yet have thousands of online followers. Particularly surprising is the fact that their parents often have no idea their child has become an online celebrity. But as Max Levine, cofounder of MC Projects—one of the many agencies that now manage young social media stars—explains, Generation X–age parents were "never told 'Yeah, just post photos and videos online and you become famous,'" so they don't realize that their child could become famous without ever leaving their bedroom.[5] What teens, even those too young to work legally, can do that many of their parents can't is effectively acquire content capital, sometimes enough to catapult them into online celebrity. While most teens use their content capital to simply gain a following as a YouTube celebrity or an Instagram influencer, some use their content capital to make inroads into established cultural fields. Perhaps the most successful example of a teen who has managed to segue her content into a cultural field is the world's most popular "Instapoet," Rupi Kaur.

Rise of the Instapoet (or How Rupi Kaur Outsold Homer)

Rupi Kaur, born in 1992, grew up in in Brampton, a suburb of Toronto. Though it is a culturally diverse place, Brampton is not exactly a cultural center. In Kaur's home suburb, you can converse with people in multiple languages, eat cuisine from around the world, and access Bollywood films as easily as you can access Hollywood films. It is not, however, the sort of place you would go to visit art galleries or museums or attend poetry readings. Nevertheless, this is where Kaur achieved a very rare form of literary success.

According to legend, Kaur was a typical suburban teenager turning out maudlin poetry in her bedroom. She did her first reading in the basement of the Punjabi community center in her home town. In 2013, she started to share her work under her own name on Tumblr and eventually Instagram. As her following and body of work grew, Kaur eventually self-published her first book, *Milk and Honey*, with CreateSpace (operated by the Amazon-owned company known as On-Demand Publishing, LLC). Unlike most literary publishers, CreateSpace isn't picky about what it publishes—they will publish any content except placeholder text. In 2017, Kaur told *Interview Magazine* that before she had published her first book, she was already gaining a following and, in her words, "doing shows and traveling and all sorts of things." With her poetry stardom on the rise, Kaur thought that producing a book might be a good idea, but as she admits, she didn't want to wait for someone to publish her work:

> I was in a creative writing course at school at the time and I went and asked my professor for some advice. She was like "I don't think you should self-publish, because it's kind of surpassing the gate-keepers in this literary community, it's not a good look. So what you want to do is perhaps take your collection, and pick a few pieces out of it and start submitting to

anthologies, and journals, and literary magazines." And so that's what I did, I was submitting my pieces to Canadian lit magazines and stuff like that and I knew I was going to face a lot of rejection naturally right? I wasn't disappointed . . . it was more so just getting very redundant, and it came to a point where I was like "Of course they are going to reject this." Reading five pieces out of *Milk and Honey* is . . . it doesn't give you the full picture. I felt what I was doing was cheating on the body of work. But I was like no this is an entire body and these pieces need to stay together because even though it's 180 poems the entire book to me is one long poem front cover to back cover. So then I was like "Ok whatever, I'm just going to self-publish."[6]

Despite not having a great deal of cultural capital (and even rejecting it outright, as implied in this interview) and despite not seeking out an established literary press in Canada or abroad, Kaur's self-published book not only did well but sold millions of copies; in time, it would land her on the *New York Times* bestseller list. Even more remarkable is the fact that her follow-up collection, *The Sun and Her Flowers*, debuted at No. 1 on the *New York Times* paperback fiction bestseller list and stayed there for months. As cultural critic Carl Wilson observes, "These are airport novel numbers, not poetry ones."[7] So what's going on?

In the world of poetry, especially Canadian poetry, Kaur's accomplishment is staggering. Poetry generally circulates in a very small market, and this is particularly true of Canadian poetry. Even well-known poets publishing with established literary presses often sell just a few hundred copies of a new poetry book. Backlisted poetry collections may sell only a few copies annually. Yet, without any connection to the Canadian literary scene or an established publisher, Kaur turned something that generally has no potential for profit not only into something profitable but also into something with a seemingly endlessly expanding audience. What separates Kaur from other poets in Canada and around the world? Sadly, her differentiator is likely not her writing (most critics agree that she is no Homer, even if she now consistently outsells him). Kaur's real differentiator appears to be her content capital.

In 2018, two editors at the *Atlantic* published an article about Kaur and other Instapoets. They summed up this new type of poetry:

> Social-media poets, using Instagram as a marketing tool, are not just artists—they're entrepreneurs. They still primarily earn money through publication and live events, but sharing their work on Instagram is now what opens up the possibility for both. Kaur, the ultimate poet-entrepreneur, said she approaches

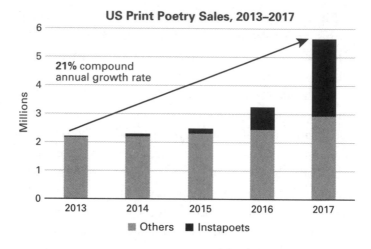

Figure 4   Instapoets' share of the US poetry market, NPD Group (2017).

poetry like "running a business." A day in the life can consist of all-day writing, touring, or, perhaps unprecedented for a poet, time in the office with her team to oversee operations and manage projects.[8]

While the *Atlantic*'s editors rightly point out that Kaur and other Instapoets have turned poetry into a business, they have also done something else—they have created an entirely new genre of poetry.

People used to talk about lyric poetry versus avant-garde poetry (let's say, the difference between someone like Billy Collins and William Burroughs). Now, some bookstores have created a special subsection for a new type of poetry—poetry produced by Instapoets. Powell's Books in Portland, Oregon, which is among the bookstores that have adopted a special classification for Instapoetry, generously explains on its website, "Instagram has emerged as an incredibly powerful platform for a new group of wordsmiths adored for their brief yet poignant poems. Many of these writers have garnered massive followings and are now exploring new mediums to showcase their work." In addition to featuring Kaur's work, Powell's Instapoet section includes a host of other popular Instapoets such as r.h. Sin and Michael Faudet. What's striking about this new classification is that the poetry's distinguishing feature has nothing to do with traditional literary classifications—for example, nation (e.g., American, Korean, or French), period (e.g., ancient, modern, or postmodern), type (e.g., haiku, epic, or language poetry), or language (e.g., Spanish, Arabic, or German). The only thing that defines Instapoetry is the fact that it originates on Instagram.

Not unlike Ulman and other visual artists whose content (selfies) has become art, for Instapoets, content (pithy little poems posted on Instagram) has become literature. While they do still publish books, for Kaur and other Instapoets, the books are, in many respects, an afterthought and just one type of merch among many other types of merch. After all, for most Instapoets, whose following comes from producing content online and not from book publications alone, the book isn't all that different from the other things they sell, including t-shirts and coffee mugs emblazoned with inspirational quotations and, in Kaur's case, a $100 pen that simply features her engraved name. In other words, the impulse to purchase the book of poetry may have less to do with a desire to read the book (after all, it's already been published online for free) and more to do with a desire to purchase a product attached to the author celebrity in question. This explains why Instapoets, unlike traditional poets, don't really need literary critics or reviewers to engage in successful position-taking in the field of cultural production. In the world of Instapoetry, the poetry doesn't need to be good or have any literary merit or be recognized by any traditional literary gatekeepers. It just needs to be copious and easily viewable on a mobile device. This is precisely why in late 2019, the *New Republic* declared Kaur the "writer of the decade." As Rumaan Alam explained, "Readers who know about poetry might think Kaur's work is dumb; those for whom Kaur is their first exposure to the medium think it profound. It doesn't matter if you believe that title of poet belongs only to the likes of Wallace Stevens or Gwendolyn Brooks. Kaur has seized it for herself."[9]

The Field of Cultural Production after Content

Summarizing what has happened to the field of cultural production in the age of content is challenging, as the effects of content on cultural production are still in progress. A few things, however, are already readily apparent.

Content Is Content Is Content

In the early 1990s, few people would have expected the *New York Times*, for example, to regularly release short documentary films. Likewise, few would have imagined turning to CNN to read rather than watch the news. In a content age, content is content is content. Printed newspapers produce short videos. Television news channels publish articles. Similarly, many book publishers now release videos and related content—hence, the growing popularity of the "book trailer." Some of this content is produced to promote printed books but, in some cases, it stands alone. As time goes on, the distinctions between mediums (e.g., film, video, audio recording, printed book) and between genres (e.g., nonfiction versus fiction or television drama versus sitcom) seem to matter less. Increasingly, what matters is simply that one is producing content and doing so at an increasingly high frequency and volume.

Everyone Is a Content Producer

In the 1990s, if you wanted to hire a writer, you hired a writer. Likewise, if you wanted to hire a filmmaker or videographer, you hired a filmmaker or videographer. Sometime in the early 2000s, the line between people who write articles versus those who make films versus those who produce videos started to blur. Now, in many contexts, all of these cultural workers are simply known as *content producers*. In this new world order, the fact that one writes as opposed to produces films or videos is insignificant. The only thing that matters is that one is engaged in some way in the production of content. But this isn't the only thing that has changed in the field of cultural production since the early 2000s.

The Line between Professional and Amateur Has Collapsed

As the distinctions between writer, filmmaker, photographer, and so on have become subsumed by the overarching category of content producer, something else has happened—a deskilling of the arts. Whereas practices such as writing, editing, filmmaking, and photography were once considered highly skilled (even if they did always have amateur participants), in the age of content, the ability to produce a lot of content increasingly seems to matter more than the ability to produce high-quality cultural products. As a result, one could argue, there has been a devaluation of skilled cultural workers and an elevation of unskilled content producers. On a work platform such as Upwork, for example, an individual with few or no credentials who promises to produce a lot of content at a very low hourly rate or fixed price might be more highly valued than a highly credentialed and experienced individual who promises to produce less content of higher quality at a higher rate per word. In today's radically restructured field of cultural production, amateurs are often preferred over professionals.

Traditional Forms of Critical Reception Have Lost Their Value

In the past, to be an artist or a writer, you needed to be recognized and supported by the artistic or literary apparatus. Artists needed gallerists and museum curators to recognize and showcase their work. Writers needed literary agents and publishers to get their work into print. Likewise, both artists and writers relied on critics, reviewers, and academics who write about art and literature to further authorize their work and affirm their identities as artists or writers. This is no longer the case. As demonstrated by an Instapoet such as Kaur, one can now successfully position oneself as a poet while bypassing all traditional forms of gatekeeping, including academics, editors at literary journals, publishers, and award juries.

Content Capital Matters More than Cultural Capital

In the age of content, even writers who continue to publish novels with traditional publishers, filmmakers who

Content begets content.

continue to produce films to be projected in theaters, and artists who continue to produce works of art for exhibit in actual galleries and museums must increasingly pay attention to the production of content. Cultural producers who, in the past, may have focused on writing books or producing films or making art must now also spend considerable time producing (or paying someone else to produce) content about themselves and their work. For novelists, for example, content about them and their work (i.e., posts, likes, mentions, and so on) translates into increased visibility. This visibility translates into more book sales, more reviews, and more invitations to read at literary festivals—and in turn, these activities lead to more content. Content begets content. As a result, in today's field of cultural production, cultural producers need to not only produce literature or art but also ensure that someone is producing content about them and their work and doing so on a constant basis.

For all of these reasons, in an age of content, the identities, output, and working conditions of cultural producers are vastly different than they were in the past. To be fair, the field of cultural production has never simply been a place where "artistic genius" was permitted to shine. Literary and artistic success have always been shaped by outside factors. Which artists are venerated, whose work is celebrated, and who can make a living as writer, artist, or performer have always been dictated by factors that exceed the work—for example, obtaining the right review at the right time in the right venue has long mattered as much as or more than what one produces. But in an age of content, what is at stake has shifted. The monopoly of power is no longer concentrated with critics, reviewers, academics, publishers, curators, and collectors. In the twenty-first century, a writer or an artist with a significant amount of content capital can thrive with or without the support of any of these gatekeepers. Naturally, many people have viewed this shift as a positive development. Why wait for a curmudgeonly editor to publish your poem or for a critic to give your book a raving review when you can take matters into your own hands and build up an influencer-level following on a social media platform like Instagram or Twitter? The problem is that in this paradigm, every writer and every artist isn't just a writer or an artist. Unless they can hire someone to do the work for them (e.g., employ an entire team to oversee their daily operations, as Kaur now does), they must also be committed to producing content about themselves and their work. They must, in effect, be both writer and content producer, both artist and content producer, and so on.

In the field of cultural production described by Bourdieu, much weight is given to acts of consecration—the preface, the favorable review, the prize, and so on. In an

In an age of content, the preface, the favorable review, and even the prize now offer diminishing returns.

age of content, though, the preface, the favorable review, and even the prize now offer diminishing returns. Cultural capital has given way to content capital. In this new field of cultural production, established forms of gatekeeping have finally crumbled and, in the process, have produced an entirely new spectrum of practices that hinge on the effectiveness of one's content strategies.

JOURNALISM AND POLITICS AFTER CONTENT

Earning $1,400 a week to churn out articles for a content farm would be considered a highly lucrative gig by anyone, even the most experienced writer. To make that much as a writer with no relevant credentials, training, or experience would generally be impossible—that is, unless you happen to work for the Internet Research Agency, one of the world's most notorious troll factories.

In 2016, when the Internet Research Agency was wreaking havoc on the US presidential election, a standard routine existed for its young recruits. Once they passed the agency's initial test by writing a sample essay on a Russian conspiracy theory dating back to the 1970s, recruits were expected to get down to business. Their first task, according to one former employee, was to create three identities on Live Journal, a popular blogging platform. One identity needed to exhibit high-quality writing skills. The other two identities were expected to demonstrate only marginal writing capabilities. Once employees had established three Live Journal identities, they were expected to start producing content—a lot of it—either in Russian or English, though the two groups of trolls were generally kept separated within the agency. During an average twelve-hour shift, writers would receive seven to eight writing prompts, always with a subject line and set of key words focusing on a topic of interest at the time—for example, President Vladimir Putin or President Barack Obama (or both together), the war in Syria, or the American role in spreading the Ebola virus. But the Internet Research Agency's real kryptonite wasn't its content but rather its ability to create the illusion that its content was popular. In addition to employing a crew of writers to produce posts on trending topics, the Internet Research Agency's computers were programmed to forward the posts to fake accounts that would, in turn, open and close the posts, generating thousands of fake page views. The tactic was designed to trick Google's PageRank algorithm and drive the agency's articles up in search results. While turning out fake news for a troll factory might sound like a terrible way to make a living, for at least some Internet Research Agency employees, it wasn't even immediately apparent that they were part of a massive propaganda machine. As one former troll factory writer told the *New York Times* in early 2018, the same week the United States Department of Justice accused the Internet Research Agency of meddling in the 2016 American presidential election, "They were just giving me money for writing."[1]

While Russia's Internet Research Agency may be one of the most notorious troll factories in the world, it is certainly not the only one. Evidence exists that troll factories in China also regularly interfere with elections in neighboring states.[2] A 2017 Harvard University study estimated that Chinese troll factories generate up to 488 million fake posts on the internet each year.[3] And while blog posts and comment pages are the bread and butter of most troll factories, troll factories have also been known to turn out different types of content. The Israel Defense Force, for example, has its own Pinterest account, which is presumably not run by military personnel.[4] Troll factories cranking out fake news (i.e., disinformation) are arguably just a symptom of a much broader problem—one that can be fully understood only by examining the restructuring of both journalism and politics in the age of content.

In addition to the world's growing number of troll factories, one doesn't need to look far to find more innocuous examples of how the content industry is eroding journalistic standards. For example, thousands of sites approved by Google News (Google's news aggregate), which purportedly circulate news items, aren't news sites at all but rather sites owned by companies looking for a clever way to sell a product or service. One content writer

I interviewed while researching this book explained how it works: "I had been writing blogs for a small software company for three years when the owner asked me to create a new site—one that he could submit and have approved by Google News. He didn't just ask me to create content for his new site but also to submit the site to Google News under my own name and email address to ensure it wouldn't look like he was simply trying to pass off his company blog as a news site, which he was."[5] The writer, who has since stopped working for this employer, confirmed that the site still exists and regularly publishes articles that appear as "news" on Google News. While this specific site, which promotes business-to-business software products, isn't as problematic as the sites connected to troll factories, it is deceptive. Worse yet, this is not an isolated problem—it extends to well-known examples, such as the *Forbes* platform.

A lot of readers, even those who are reasonably educated, often assume the articles they read on *Forbes* are at least somewhat newsworthy. After all, many of the articles present themselves as news and Google's algorithm classifies them as news. In fact, much of the content that appears on *Forbes* is written by Forbes "members." Members belong to a "Forbes Council" such as its "Finance Council," "Coaching Council," or "Technology Council." For a fee, just over $1,000 annually, one not only gets to become a member of a Forbes Council but also to post articles on the Forbes platform once or twice a month. While members can't actively promote their own company, service, or product (an editor will request an edit if a member is bold enough to overtly plug his or her own business), their "thought leadership" on the platform still helps raise their profile and legitimize their services and products. These articles aren't examples of journalism or even authored op-eds (most Forbes members hire ghostwriters to produce their posts) but rather are cleverly masked examples of branded content.

On the surface, comparing a *Forbes* article offering tips on how to become a better executive to disinformation leaked out of a Russian troll factory may seem unfair. After all, while the *Forbes* content may be misleading, the Russian troll factory content is damaging to democracy itself. Still, one would be naïve to assume that the former isn't connected to the latter. Relatively innocuous content like a *Forbes* article blurs the line between opinion and reputable journalism and, in the process, it creates an opportunity for more damaging forms of content production to take root. After all, in both instances, we're confronted with content masquerading as news. Also, both are forms of interference with the truth. Forbes interferes with the truth because it is a site where articles published by staff writers run alongside thousands of "pay-to-play" opinion pieces and not enough is done to help readers understand the difference between the site's news and branded content. An article generated by a troll factory interferes with the truth on a more intentional and dangerous level. When combined, these two types of content have already had a profound impact on what passes as journalism and what counts as the truth, as well as on the political landscape in the twenty-first century. Unfortunately, too few readers fully recognize or understand this shift.

Journalism in an Age of Content

In *Democracy without Journalism? Confronting the Misinformation Society*, media studies scholar Victor Pickard outlines the three fundamental "media failures" that upended the 2016 presidential election in the United States. First, he suggests that excessive commercialism resulted in "facile coverage of the election that emphasized entertainment over information."[6] Second, Pickard points to the misinformation circulating on social media platforms, especially Facebook. Third, he argues that we started to witness the consequences of the structural collapse of professional journalism during the 2016 US presidential election. Among other things, Pickard notes, since 2000, print newsrooms have lost more than half of their employees, which has led not only to fewer professional writers and editors but also to fewer fact-checkers.[7]

While Pickard's focus is on the United States, and specifically the 2016 presidential election, the media failures he explores are by no means isolated to one nation or one election. What he is ultimately laying out is how journalism has been radically upended in the age of content. In the United States and around the world, journalism hasn't just come to be viewed as content. Content with no journalistic integrity at all has increasingly come to be viewed as journalism. The effects—not simply on journalism as a profession but on democracy—are arguably catastrophic, and the full impact on journalism and politics may not be fully understood for years. Still, a few things have already become clearly apparent.

The Content Industry Has Negatively Impacted Professional Journalism

That print newsrooms have lost half of their employees since 2000 isn't entirely surprising. After all, most people no longer rely on printed newspapers but rather on digital platforms to access the news. Consequently, the United States lost over 1,800 daily and weekly newspapers between 2004 and 2018.[8] However, this doesn't mean people aren't accessing the news.

In the United States and around the world, journalism hasn't just come to be viewed as content. Content with no journalistic integrity at all has increasingly come to be viewed as journalism.

As traditional print-based media sources have gone into decline, demand for other types of content, even news content, has surged. Audiences who once may have been content to read the news each morning increasingly expect new articles on an hourly basis and even more frequently. A 2018 study by the American Press Institute found that 59 percent of Americans look at the news several times a day and 6 percent look several times an hour—a practice that would not have been possible a generation ago.[9] In a sense, we've rapidly pivoted from a culture of the daily newspaper to a culture of the notification. This pivot has changed both traditional journalistic institutions (e.g., printed newspapers) and their digital counterparts. Between 2010 and 2016, for example, the number of stories, graphics, interactives, and blog posts published in the *New York Times* spiked 35 percent. This increase is nothing compared to the spike in production seen on new media platforms such as Buzzfeed during roughly the same period. Buzzfeed, one of the many digital journalism sites that has gained prominence in the age of content, was publishing just 914 posts per month in 2012 but over 6,300 posts per month only four years later.[10] Much of this content is also notably different from the type of content that once dominated printed dailies. As the demand for content has surged, more published articles, even in reputable newspapers, have taken the form of opinion pieces. While some of these opinion-based articles are written by professional journalists, many are not. Hard news—that is, serious, fact-based reporting on politics, foreign affairs, and so on—still exists, but it is no longer necessarily the default.

The Content Industry Has Expanded the Commercial Influence on Journalism

Journalism has long been driven by advertising revenue, but over the past two decades, several things have changed. Historically, most local newspapers relied on local advertising revenue and subscription fees. With the rise of digital content, both sources of income have been compromised. Twenty-first century readers are far less likely to pay for access to news, including local news. As a result, subscription-based publications have suffered. Also, local businesses no longer need to pay to place advertisements in local newspapers in order to find new customers, as creating a free Facebook or Instagram account is often a more effective way to reach potential customers. In addition, revenues from classified advertisements have all but disappeared. After all, if you want to hire a tutor, sell your canoe, or rent out your spare room, you're now far more likely to post an advertisement online for free than to take out an advertisement in your local newspaper.

As potential sources of revenue have disappeared, many smaller newspapers have collapsed, been bought up by larger regional or national conglomerates, or survived, but only online. While moving from print to an exclusively digital format has enabled some smaller local dailies or weeklies to survive, the move online has brought its own set of unique challenges. With advertising decisions being made by algorithms not people, advertisers rarely choose to run advertisements targeting micro markets, especially if those micro markets are known to be home to people with little disposal income. As a result, even newspapers that have ceased their print-based operations typically struggle to remain viable online, and those that do survive typically only do so with a skeletal staff capable of doing little original reporting. As Pickard observes in *Democracy without Journalism?*, the value of the current US media system (and one might argue, the current media system around the world) is now "largely determined by ratings, clicks, and profitability."[11]

The Content Industry and Its Economic Model Have Expanded News Deserts

For all the reasons previously outlined, the past two decades have also seen the rapid expansion of *news deserts*—regions with no access to local news reporting at all. Take, for example, Ann Arbor, Michigan. Despite being home to more than 120,000 citizens, its only surviving daily newspaper shut down in 2009. Fortunately, in Ann Arbor, the gap has been filled by its university's student newspaper, *Michigan Daily*, which reports not only on university events but also on municipal politics and local arrests.[12] In many other regions, though, local reporting is now

Do You Live in a News Desert?

In the US, 200 counties do not have a local newspaper.
Half of all counties—1,528—have ony one newspaper, usually a weekly.

■ No newspapers
■ One newspaper

Figure 5 "Do You Live in a News Desert?" Map courtesy of UNC Hussman School of Journalism and Media.

completely absent. While all areas are impacted, rural areas have been especially hard hit. More than 500 newspapers closed or merged in rural areas across the United States between 2004 and 2018, and similar trends can be found in countries around the world.[13] Worse yet, growing evidence exists that news deserts aren't just bad for journalism; they are bad for democracy.

As James T. Hamilton and Fiona Morgan explain in their 2018 study on the relationship between income and information access, while voters need news to help them cast informed votes, "The degree to which information gets produced . . . depends on the value a producer places on influencing the decisions people make in the marketplace, workplace, and voting booth. People with low incomes will get less information supplied to meet their needs because they are less likely to be a valued consumer, worker, audience member, or voter targeted for persuasion."[14] Thus, in an age of content, both reputable newspapers and content farm sites now rely on a remarkably similar financial model. Since advertisers make more money targeting consumers in large and wealthy markets, people living in smaller and poorer markets are also less likely to have access to relevant news. In a democracy, this leaves some voters—namely, those with the least economic power— less able to make informed decisions.

The absence of local news, however, doesn't necessarily mean that people aren't reading. In many cases, people without access to local news are increasingly relying on alternative sources, including the news feeds found on social media sites.[15] While younger Americans are most likely to rely on social media sites as their primary news source, people in news deserts across age demographics are also frequently forced, by necessity, to do so.[16] As a result, they are more likely to access aggregated news sources. Relying on aggregated sources can leave one more likely to end up living in a "filter bubble"—a term coined by internet activist and entrepreneur Eli Pariser to describe the growing tendency of readers to be exposed only to viewpoints that already support their own views.[17]

The Content Industry Is Misunderstood and Media Literacy Hasn't Caught Up

Given the growing reliance on social media feeds as a news source and the preponderance of fake news and opinion-driven news, the need for media literacy is pressing. Yet media literacy—the general reader's ability to read, evaluate, and critically engage with the news—has lagged behind the current era of media change.

As already noted, even relatively educated readers frequently don't realize that articles run on sites such as *Forbes* or the *Huffington Post* are often written by contributors who either share their content for free or, in the case of *Forbes*, pay for the privilege. Worse yet, many readers fail to recognize that many of these articles carry little or no newsworthy content. But sadly, a large majority of adult readers in the United States also struggle to separate opinion from fact. A 2018 Pew Research Study found that only about a quarter of adult Americans were capable of doing so.[18] This low level of basic media literacy is especially troubling given that op-eds and even branded content increasingly share space with hard-news headlines.

The Search Engine Optimization of Politics

In an era when access to information is increasingly determined by one's consumer status, more buying power means more access to relevant news. This inequity creates an increasingly uneven playing field for voters, but it isn't the only thing that has changed since the early 2000s. To fully understand how the content industry has impacted not only journalism but also politics, we need to consider two other factors: the monetization of political content (in some cases, by people with no interest in politics at all) and the content strategies of political campaigns.

Clicks, Views, and the Monetization of Political Content
On November 16, 2016, late-night talk show host Stephen Colbert had a special request for a specific group of teens: "Hey, Macedonian teenagers. Why can't you do normal teenager stuff? Knock it off!" That an American late-night talk show host was speaking directly to a particular group of teens is unusual. The fact that the statement was addressed to a group of Macedonian teenagers made it even stranger. But this wasn't a normal time—it was just eight days after the election of President Donald Trump, and it was becoming increasingly apparent that a lot of surprising things had already happened, including unprecedented interference by outside individuals and organizations in the US presidential election.

Alongside large-scale operations like the Internet Research Agency, several smaller but not insignificant players had influenced the 2016 US presidential election, including a group of Macedonian teenagers who were reportedly more interested in owning fancy cars than manipulating US politics. As several post-election investigations revealed, the teens had discovered that they didn't have to settle for the average Macedonian monthly salary, which is equivalent to about $371 in US dollars. Instead, they could do what other enterprising Macedonians had already done—buy a domain, build a website, and generate revenue on Google AdSense.

Consider, for example, Boris (not his real name), who was featured in a 2017 article published in *Wired* magazine. Although Boris spoke little English, he didn't need to be fluent to launch a website featuring passable English-language content and start turning a profit. First, he did what most domain owners do—he bought a few domains from GoDaddy, including GossipKnowledge.com and DailyInterestingThings.com, linked them to a couple of WordPress sites, and then started to cut and paste English-language articles (all pilfered from other sources) into his sites. Shortly after he started his sites, he happened to post a fake news article about Trump slapping a man at a rally. The article garnered 800 views—a statistic that drove up the seventeen-year-old's monthly AdSense revenues to $150. Assuming that more Trump-themed articles might be a good idea and get him closer to buying his first BMW, Boris started to specialize in American politics. While his NewYorkTimesPolitics.com site had to be taken down (after a cease-and-desist order), his Politics Hall.com site persisted and soon gained a solid following. As reported in *Wired*, between August and November,

Boris made close to $16,000 from just two pro-Trump websites. But he wasn't alone. His small town was home to fifty-five registered pro-Trump websites.[19]

While Boris and his friends may have done more political damage than most people hoping to make a bit of extra cash on AdSense, what they were doing was neither original nor unique. They recognized that to make a lot of money from a website, the content needs to appeal to a large swath of readers. Home to more than 300 million people, the United States is already a large market, and as a world power, its elections tend to be of interest to people around the world. As a result, publishing articles, especially politically divisive ones, about an upcoming US presidential election is a sure way to attract a lot of readers, especially if the articles are search-engine-optimized. What may be good for business, however, is very bad for democracy. Indeed, fake news has flourished in the age of content not only because people intent on interfering with elections can now easily do so (as demonstrated by the impact of troll factories) but also because people with little or no interest at all in politics (people like Boris and his friends in Veles, Macedonia) have discovered that they can easily capitalize on the production and circulation of fake news. In addition to the disinformation and misinformation that are intentionally circulated to interfere with elections, a certain percentage is being circulated simply to generate enough clicks and views to yield a high return on AdSense. Still, fake news isn't the only political content in circulation.

When Big-Seed Marketing Meets Political Campaigns

Thirty years ago, most political campaigns sought to communicate a single message—ideally encapsulated by a memorable slogan—and to circulate the message via just a few forms of communication: printed newspaper ads, flyers, lawn signs and billboards, in-person conversations, and cold calls. For this reason, most political campaigns were not only laser-focused on just one or two key messages but also intensely localized—so localized, you could often call an election before it happened based on the number of signs banged into front lawns alone. In an age of content, localized tactics for securing votes have given way to a new set of tactics that largely pivot around the production, search engine optimization, and circulation of content across multiple digital platforms.

Consider, for example, the surprising success of Alexandria Ocasio-Cortez, who knocked out a longstanding Democratic incumbent in her district to become one of the youngest US Congress members in history. Amazingly, Ocasio-Cortez, who had been working as a bartender before becoming a Congress member, achieved this feat with a much smaller campaign budget than her opponent's. What she lacked in campaign funding, she made up for with an enviable content strategy. BuzzFeed writer

Charlie Warzel suggests that Ocasio-Cortez's success ultimately rested on her ability to control her own narrative, connect with voters, and ensure she stayed on everyone's radar, even her opponent's. "Constant content creation," Warzel observes, "forces your opponent to respond to *you*."[20] Since being elected, Ocasio-Cortez has continued to use this content strategy to her advantage. This means that rather than being associated with a single and repeatable message, Ocasio-Cortez continues to focus on producing a constant stream of new content. On a single day, she might publish digital content that features her explaining a complex political concept, making mac and cheese in her kitchen, taking selfies with people on the street, or posing with the stars of a Netflix series. Rather than focus on making a single message go viral, Ocasio-Cortez seems to be a natural pro at bringing "big-seed marketing" to politics.

Big-seed marketing is a concept introduced by Microsoft researcher Duncan Watts and digital publisher Jonah Peretti. In a 2007 *Harvard Business Review* article, they explained that big-seed marketing combines the power of viral marketing with the power of traditional media. Viral marketing, Watts and Peretti note, "assumes that one starts with a seed of individuals who spread a message by infecting their friends, where the expected number of new infectious people generated by each existing one is called the 'reproduction rate,' or R. When R is greater than 1, each person who gets the message will, on average, spread it to more than one additional person, who then does the same thing, and so on, leading to exponential growth in the number of people who receive it—an epidemic." Where the analogy breaks down is when one starts to take scale into account. Unlike an infectious disease, after all, companies—and political campaigns—can control the size of their seed. Rather than starting with a small seed and hoping a message goes viral, they can start with a large seed. The beauty of big-seed marketing is that it doesn't rely on luck or a celebrity endorsement. As Watts and Peretti observe, "Big-seed marketing harnesses the power of large numbers of ordinary people."[21]

Both Ocasio-Cortez and one of her most famous rivals, Donald Trump, arguably managed to do this on opposite sides of the political spectrum during the 2016 US election. Still, scale only works with the right type of content. In Ocasio-Cortez's case, the ability to speak the language of many her supporters—for example, her effective use of emojis and memes—has proven as essential as her ability to take complicated political concepts and break them down into social-media-size bites. In Trump's case, provocative tweets about political rivals proved especially effective. While Ocasio-Cortez's and Trump's content is marked by stark political contrast (and a different level of tolerance for fake news), their content strategies—lots of content, rolled out 24/7, that is accessible to a range of audiences—are surprisingly similar.

Fake News and the Content Industry

To suggest that the content industry produced the problem of fake news would be misleading. Disinformation and misinformation existed long before content farms and troll factories. However, disinformation and misinformation have become more prevalent in the age of content, because for these problems to flourish, certain conditions needed to be in place—and the content industry provided these conditions.

Reduced Cost of Producing and Circulating News Content

In the digital age, anyone can buy a domain, create a website, and start publishing content, including content that masquerades as news. Thanks to content farms, which often pay writers just a few dollars per article, producing a lot of content at a low cost is possible, even without a huge start-up budget. A team of professional journalists is no longer needed. But the ability to turn out a lot of content at little cost is just one reason fake news has been able to flourish since the early 2000s.

Trusted News Sources Are No Longer the Only or Most Popular News Sources

In the 1990s, most people accessed news from just a few sources; for example, they might have had subscriptions to the *New York Times* and a local weekly newspaper and watched the nightly news on CBS. Three decades later, some people still subscribe to printed dailies or week-lies or watch nightly newscasts delivered by established broadcasters, but this is no longer the norm. Many people now access news (or what they perceive to be news) via aggregates or the newsfeeds on one or more social me-dia platforms (e.g., Twitter, Facebook, or Instagram). In this context, articles from established news sources be-come part of an endless stream of news-like content that may also include articles from new and emerging digital sources (e.g., BuzzFeed), platforms dominated by branded content (e.g., *Forbes*), articles that have been classified as "news" on Google News that may or may not be newswor-thy, as well as fake news.

Fake News Generates Clicks and Views

Propaganda has long existed, but in the past, one generally had to pay to circulate it or recruit people to one's cause so they would circulate it for free. Today, some people still pay to have propaganda produced and put into circulation. Propaganda that takes the form of fake news, however, also tends to generate a high number of clicks and views. As such, fake news has expanded in the age of content not simply because it is less expensive to produce and circulate but also because it has proven to be a popular way to gen-erate revenue on platforms such as Google AdSense. After

Fake news has expanded
in the age of content
not simply because
it is less expensive to
produce and circulate
but also because it has
proven to be a popular
way to generate revenue
on platforms such as
Google AdSense.

all, while a website offering advice on how to do home repairs can be lucrative over time, if you want to make money quickly, a website offering salacious articles about a presidential candidate's sex scandals is nearly always a better business proposition.

The content industry has already had a far-reaching impact on journalism and politics. As suggested throughout this chapter, as the content industry has grown, many traditional news producers, especially on the print side of the industry, have struggled to survive. Yet people are still accessing news—or what they perceive to count as news. There is growing evidence that thanks to digital media and mobile devices, people may even be spending more time than ever before engaging with the news daily. The problem is that the quality of these engagements is highly questionable. As discussed earlier, the number of people who access news solely or primarily through aggregates continues to rise, with more people now getting their news on platforms such as Facebook, Twitter, or Instagram where factual news items tend to be mixed with branded content and sometimes misinformation. In theory, sourcing one's news from an aggregate would not be a significant problem if everyone had the ability to tell the difference between vetted professional journalism and other types of content, but there is evidence that this is not the case (some studies have found that as few as one in four adults is able to consistently separate fact from opinion). But this doesn't mean nothing can be done in response. Efforts to identify and slow the growth of news deserts, such as by finding ways to make regional reporting economically viable, are a start. Expanding media literacy (as this book seeks to do) is another important part of this effort.

CONTENT AUTOMATION

Assuming content is here to stay, what does the future hold? Will content production become increasingly automated? Will the content industry continue to thrive without human producers or consumers? If so, who will be left on the sidelines as bots carry out the research and production and even decide which bot-produced article or film is worthy of being put into circulation?

The Evolution of Content Automation

Content automation may be the future of content, but it is by no means an entirely new concept; it is as old as computing itself. In the early 1950s, pioneering British computer scientist Christopher Strachey programmed a computer to generate love letters.[1] Strachey's automated love letters may not have been persuasive, but they did represent a first step toward content automation. A decade later, Jean Baudot, an enterprising professor at the University of Montreal, programmed a computer to write poetry. Professor Baudot's experiment, *La machine à écrire*, was published as a limited-edition printed book—a curious artifact, antiquated even for its time, featuring uncut pages.[2] Experiments in content automation have also long found a home in other fields, including music. Computational compositions date back to Iannis Xenakis's experiments in the 1950s and, from the 1970s onward, continued to be developed by researchers and musicians such as David Cope.[3] While these early experiments are significant in their own rights (and by no means represent a comprehensive list), none is particularly well known. As conceptually interesting as the products of these early experiments in content automation were, they failed to respond to a general audience's need to be entertained. Over the past two decades, however, content automation has been upended by two developments.

First, since the late 1990s, natural language processing (NLP)—the ability of machines to read, understand, decipher, and even reproduce human languages—has undergone a series of rapid advancements. Thanks to the growing availability of large data sets and the machines needed to process large data sets, NLP is starting to appear a lot more "natural," and as a result, is driving improvements in the quality of machine-generated content. Second, and perhaps more important, content is no longer produced simply to be read or listened to or viewed by humans. While a great deal of content is still produced for human consumption, it may also be produced simply for the sake of circulation. For this reason, content is under no obligation to tell a story or communicate a message or convey an emotion, or to do any of these things well. With humans increasingly on the sidelines, whether or not automated content passes the Turing test (i.e., has the appearance of being human-generated) simply doesn't matter.

With content automation now entering a new phase, it is no longer something of interest only to computer programmers, experimental poets, and avant-garde composers. As algorithms become increasingly capable of turning out readable texts, even if they are far from perfect, and as more content circulates simply for the sake of circulation, all sorts of content—from news to television and film scripts to genre fiction—are about to be transformed. Understandably, this may sound sinister. After all, who wants a machine to write their front-page news or a script for their favorite sitcom or soap opera? Yet some people are convinced that content automation may hold the potential to fix some of the problems that have already been created by the content industry.

Content Automation as a Response to News Deserts

In 2017, PA Media Group, which bills itself as the largest content provider in the United Kingdom and Ireland, launched an initiative intended to help support local reporting. The plan had nothing to do with creating more jobs for local reporters or funneling money back into local newspapers; instead, the content provider launched RADAR (Reporters and Data and Robots) with a multimillion-dollar grant from Google's Digital News Initiative (DNI) Innovation Fund. PA Media Group hoped their initiative might enhance local reporting by getting robots to do some of the work once done by regional reporters. The scheme was never devoid of human input. When the initiative launched, for example, one of RADAR's human journalists would write a few story templates, and the actual stories were created by pulling data from over 391 regional authorities (primarily open-source government data sets).[4] Just two years after RADAR's launch, the *Columbia Journalism Review* reported that the program was already turning out 8,000 stories monthly with a team of only five journalists, two editors, and an unspecified number of bots.[5]

At the time of RADAR's launch in 2017, the PA Media Group insisted that the scheme wasn't just another attempt to displace human reporters. As one RADAR editor told the BBC, "Skilled human journalists will still be vital in the process, but RADAR allows us to harness artificial intelligence to scale up to a volume of local stories that would be impossible to provide manually."[6] Yet, while RADAR was launched as a mash-up of humans and robots, there is reason to question whether this human-computer collaboration will persist over time. In late May 2020, just three years after RADAR's launch, the *Guardian* reported that approximately twenty-seven people employed by the PA Media Group (albeit not the same employees working on the RADAR project) were being replaced with bots. All of the employees had been working on contracts for Microsoft's MSN website and its Edge browser. While they weren't engaged in original reporting, they selected stories produced by other news sources, and edited content and headlines for Microsoft's news sites. After partnering with PA Media Group for several years, Microsoft decided to hand over its news service fully to AI.[7] As one sacked employee told the *Seattle Times* on the condition of anonymity, "[The site's] been semi-automated for a few months but now it's full speed ahead. It's demoralizing to think machines can replace us but there you go."[8]

PA Media Group's RADAR experiment is certainly not the only example of content automation's growing presence in journalism. Since 2017, major newspapers and digital content platforms around the world have brought bots on board to help scale their content production. The

Washington Post introduced readers to Heliograf in 2017, initially to help the newspaper provide coverage of all DC-area high school football games.[9] In 2018, Reuters introduced Lynx Insight, which not only combs through massive amounts of data to compile relevant insights but also writes sentences that reporters can drag and drop into stories.[10] Not surprisingly, digital content producers like *Forbes* have also turned to bots—*Forbes*'s staff writers rely on a bot named Bertie.

Whether content automation ever takes over the production of local news or solves the problem of news deserts is yet to be seen. What seems nearly certain is that over time another contemporary journalistic problem— fake news—is likely to get a huge boost from content automation.

In 2019, OpenAI, a San Francisco-based research institute, set out to develop what they described as a general-purpose language algorithm. In the process, they realized that the algorithm was capable of generating remarkably convincing fake news. In the end, OpenAI held back the release of their algorithm because it was too dangerous.[11] Despite OpenAI's ethical decision to not release its algorithm, it is only a matter of time before someone else develops and releases a similar algorithm, making possible the production of reasonably convincing disinformation and misinformation without the support or cost of troll factories.

Automated Entertainment Content

News agencies are not the only organizations that may be invested in the automated production of content. In 2018, Netflix produced 700 original television shows and 80 films. To put this into context, four decades earlier, established television broadcasters like ABC and CBS were producing only about twenty-five to thirty original television programs each year. Most of these shows ran only once a week during the regular season. By contrast, Netflix releases new content across its various entertainment categories from drama to documentary to crime to comedy on a daily basis. According to one estimate, Netflix's yearly original content added up to just over 1,537 hours in 2018 (for anyone who is interested in binge watching, that would offer about 64 days of nonstop television watching) and over 2,769 hours in 2019 (equivalent to about 115 days of nonstop television watching). If Netflix continues to increase its content at this rate, it is on track to offer 365 full days of new content annually by 2022.[12] Whether Netflix is responding to an actual consumer demand or a perceived consumer demand, or is just keeping its shareholders happy, is debatable. What is clear is that Netflix's executives aren't spending much time agonizing over the types of programs in which to invest. The company has a long history of relying on AI to make decisions about what types of content to produce. Given the company's success, one might conclude that letting AI dictate their content has already proven to be an incredibly successful strategy. In the future, however, AI may do more than inform Netflix's decisions about what types of content to produce.

As of 2020, no successful feature-length film or television series has been written by bots. As in journalism, the transition from human- to computer-generated content will likely be long and uneven, and will initially entail a lot of human-machine collaboration. Still, it seems inevitable that content automation will eventually upend at least some aspects of script production. In 2018, award-winning director Kevin McDonald directed a sixty-second Lexus commercial using a dialogue-free script produced by IBM's AI platform known as Watson. McDonald would later tell the *Los Angeles Times*, "It's only a matter of time where the formula of what makes up a great story, a great character can be learned by a computer."[13] But is it really? McDonald's script didn't even have any dialogue. Could a longer script with dialogue—let's say, a script for an ongoing television series or feature-length film—also be automated?

While we may not be there yet, several companies are attempting to gain a foothold in the automated script market. ScriptBook, which currently offers script analysis services, is likely uninterested in script analysis as an endgame. Rather, ScriptBook and its competitors are eagerly collecting and analyzing film and television scripts to help train bots to produce scripts without any human intervention. Whether or not they will be successful anytime soon is unclear, but the writing is already on the wall: the production of some content—for example, television commercials, film trailers, and lowbrow and high-volume genres like soap operas—seems likely to eventually become at least partially automated.

But if bots can potentially write scripts for television or film, could a bot also produce literature? Could the Booker Prize shortlist eventually find Zadie Smith pitted against IBM's Watson? Or what about genre fiction? Could Harlequin Romance, which already publishes a massive amount of content each month (about 120 unique titles), lower its cost and increase its content production by handing over some or all of its writing to romance-writing bots?

To date, content automation of literature hasn't progressed much since the 1960s. In 2017, writer and researcher Ross Goodwin set out on a road trip from Brooklyn to New Orleans with a bunch of data collection devices, including a surveillance system, a microphone, and an outdated GPS unit, attached to the roof of his Cadillac. Along the way, Goodwin's devices observed, listened to, and tracked his journey and fed all of the data into a laptop. The result is a book called *1 the Road*.[14] Upon its release, it was billed by its French publisher as "the first real book written by an AI" (though even Goodwin has contested this claim). Reviews suggest that Goodwin's novel—or as it was described in a 2018 article in the *Atlantic*, "novel" (in scare quotes)—shares more in common with the curious writing experiments overseen by the likes of Strachey and Baudot in the 1950s to 1960s than it does with the type of fiction one finds for sale at the average airport bookstore.[15] While Goodwin's novel is the result of more advanced technologies than those of Strachey and Baudot, it still fails to meet the expectations most readers have of novels.

Somewhat surprisingly, attempts to turn out genre fiction also appear far from successful, even if one might suspect bots to be potentially good at creating formulaic stories. In 2017, sci-fi writer and computational scientist Elle O'Brien tried feeding 20,000 Harlequin Romance titles into a neural network designed to generate similar book titles. The result was amusing but not necessarily market-friendly. While some readers might be intrigued by a book with a title like *The Baby Doctor Seduction* or *The Sheikh's Convenient Desires*, none of these bot-generated romance titles seem likely to appeal to diehard romance readers or to make the final cut at Harlequin.[16]

The Future of Content

Even if content automation is still a work in progress, content is already an integral part of the world's economy, cultures, and politics. If content production becomes increasingly automated, then, a lot will be at stake. The livelihood of people working across sectors from journalism to education, the integrity of cultural production, and even the future of democratic elections may all be on the line. Content may be something few people fully understand or ever take the time to contemplate, but this still-fuzzy concept that has quickly gained currency and seeped into our vernacular is far more insidious than many expect. Still, content and the content industry are not necessarily out of our control yet. Content—and along with it, content producers, content providers, content automation, and so on—may be here to stay, but a few critical interventions hold the possibility of mitigating its least desirable effects.

Content Literacy
Above all, it is urgent that people of all ages and across all sectors better understand content—what it is, how it is produced, by whom, and for what ends. If more people understood how and why content is produced and how it touches nearly every aspect of their lives, they would presumably be able to start making smarter decisions about how they engage with it. Content wouldn't disappear, but the effects of some problems brought about by the rise of the content industry, such as disinformation and misinformation, might at least be contained. To be successful, content literacy will need to be taught on a mass scale in

K–12 schools, colleges, and the workplace, and even be promoted through public awareness campaigns. Finding ways to carry out large-scale content literacy campaigns without relying on the content industry, however, will prove virtually impossible. Ironically, content producers and providers will likely need to be part of any widespread effort to help the general public understand the effects of their industry.

Content Regulation
To mitigate at least some of the negative impacts of the content industry, regulation will need to increase. In some regions of the world, including the European Union, efforts are already underway to increase the regulation of content (e.g., by regulating any content that appears to support or incite terrorist activities). In the United States, where most of the world's largest technology companies are based, content regulation appears bound to remain a point of contention. A series of events in early 2020 offered insight into the polarized nature of this battle.

In February 2020, Facebook—after several years of increased scrutiny for its failure to regulate content—released a white paper on the subject. In "Charting a Way Forward: Online Content Regulation," Monica Bickert, Facebook's vice president of content policy, maintained that content regulation ultimately has one key goal—"to reduce harmful speech while preserving free expression."

It is urgent that people of all ages and across all sectors better understand content—what it is, how it is produced, by whom, and for what ends.

Bickert outlined several potential ways to achieve this goal: "(1) holding internet companies accountable for having certain systems and procedures in place, (2) requiring companies to meet specific performance targets when it comes to content that violates their policies, or (3) requiring companies to restrict specific forms of speech, even if the speech is not illegal."[17] Not surprisingly, Bickert and Facebook concluded that the first and least prescriptive approach is the best approach to content regulation. Following the publication of Facebook's "Charting a Way Forward," Twitter took a very different stance on content regulation when it first added "check the facts" warnings to several of President Donald Trump's tweets and eventually, in early 2021, pushed President Trump off the platform altogether. In the United States, where conflicting interpretations of the First Amendment make content regulation subject to ongoing debate, guidelines for regulating content seem likely to continue to be contested.

Content Resistance

Alongside content literacy and content regulation, the future world of content might be structured by a small but persistent resistance movement—a movement of people who actively reject the idea that all communication and cultural production is now mere content. These people won't be neo-Luddites; they will appreciate and support media that can't be easily monetized by the content industry. Content resisters, and they are already among us, will be people who celebrate old and forgotten mediums—for example, people who collect and even cut vinyl records, print books on letterpress machines, and favor photocopied zines over blogs and vlogs. These content resisters will never bring the content industry to its knees. Content and the content industry are here to stay; indeed, much of the damage has already been done. These content resisters, however, may find a way to disrupt the flow of content by reminding us that one can still cut an album or publish a printed collection of poetry or engage in a public debate without handing anything over to the content industry. Content resisters will stubbornly reject the temptation to accumulate content capital. They will approach communication on content management platforms as only one choice among many others. Ultimately, they will refuse to turn every communicative act into another addition to the pool.

GLOSSARY

Branded content
Content produced through a sponsored or paid partnership between a brand and a media platform (e.g., a digital publication). Branded content doesn't directly sell a commodity (e.g., running shoes) but rather is sponsored by a company that communicates a separate message (e.g., female empowerment). Rather than focus on selling a product or service, branded content seeks to generate brand loyalty. While branded content has certainly expanded in the digital age, it is not necessarily new.

Clickbait
Any online content (e.g., a written article, a video, or an interactive) produced solely for the purpose of generating revenue with views and clicks. Clickbait uses provocative headlines and hyperlinks to encourage readers and viewers to click through as many pages as possible to generate more views and clicks, which is how platforms such as Google AdSense calculate advertising revenue.

Commons-based peer production
A cooperative model that encourages large numbers of people to come together to solve problems. Legal scholar Yochai Benkler coined the term to describe open-source software (e.g., Linux), but open-source software is just one example of how people with diverse skills can now come together to build or improve a product or service.

Content
Generally refers to anything that circulates online, be it a text, an image, a video, a sound file, or an interactive. While some content conveys a message, shares information, or tells a story, content doesn't need to communicate anything at all. Content is often produced simply to circulate and not to communicate.

Content automation
The use of natural-language-processing technologies either to remove or to reduce the need for human intervention in the life cycle of content. Many established newspapers already deploy some form of content automation. The

Washington Post's Heliograf and *Bloomberg News*'s Cyborg are two examples of content automation technologies that at least partially automate content production.

Content capital
A form of capital, analogous to social, symbolic, or cultural capital, acquired through the production of content about oneself or one's work. In a digital era, the success of artists and writers, for example, increasingly rests on their content capital or online assets. Such assets include but are not limited to the amount of content that exists about oneself online and the number of one's followers on social media platforms.

Content creation
The act of producing digital content of any kind (text, image, video, etc.) for any online platform. Content creation is usually associated with the work of content creators (e.g., writers, videographers, game designers, and so on).

Content development
The act of developing digital content of any kind (text, image, video, etc.) for any online platform. Content development is generally carried out by a team that includes not only content creators (e.g., writers, videographers, etc.) but also content strategists, web developers, designers, and engineers.

Content director
Anyone who oversees the content strategy for a company. Content directors use data such as audience metrics to help make decisions about the type of content that is most popular. Content directors are employed by all types of digital platforms (publishers, video-streaming platforms, etc.).

Content editor
Anyone who edits digital content. The term is used to describe individuals who edit texts, videos, and other types of digital content.

Content farm (or content mill)
A large pool of content producers who generally work remotely and may include writers, photographers, videographers, and anyone else who is engaged in the production of content.

Content management system

Any software application used to manage the creation of content. WordPress, which is used around the world to build and update websites, is a well-known example of a content management system.

Content producer

Anyone who produces content for an online platform. Content producers may be writers, photographers, filmmakers, television producers, or recording artists. The medium in which they work is irrelevant so long as they produce some type of content for a digital platform.

Content provider

Any company that produces digital content of any kind. Educational publishers (e.g., Cengage), streaming platforms (e.g., Netflix), or digital news sources (e.g., BuzzFeed) are all examples of content providers.

Content regulation

Any effort to regulate content, including efforts carried out by content platforms (e.g., Twitter's decision to place warnings on posts that do not meet their rules) or governments (e.g., the EU's Terrorist Content Regulation, which gives the EU the power to force content management platforms and content providers to police any content seen to support terrorism).

Content strategy

The planning, production, or distribution of content. Although it is generally associated with marketing campaigns, in a digital age, many individuals also have a content strategy. Successful artists and writers, for example, frequently have a content strategy to promote themselves and their work, as do many elected officials.

Content writer

Anyone who produces text-based content for one or more online sites.

Convergence culture

The new media landscape opened up by participatory media—a space where old and new media, analog and digital media, and grassroots and corporate media appear to collide. As Henry Jenkins observed in his 2006 book on the

subject, convergence culture enables new forms of participation and collaboration, and shifts traditional power relations.

Disinformation
False or misleading information that is deliberately put into circulation. Because the content industry facilitates the production and distribution of
content at a low cost, it also enables the easy and widespread circulation of
disinformation.

Fake news
Content that masquerades as news but fails to meet basic journalistic standards. It is synonymous with *disinformation* (the deliberate production and
circulation of false or misleading information).

Filter bubble
The growing tendency of readers to be exposed only to viewpoints that support their own views (a term coined by internet activist and entrepreneur Eli
Pariser). Facebook's personalized news stream is frequently associated with
the creation of filter bubbles, but all news streams that select news articles for
readers based on their previous online behaviors can be seen as a contributing factor.

Google AdSense
An automated advertising platform, launched by Google in 2003, that enables
domain owners to easily place advertisements on any website. Google shares
a percentage of the advertising revenue with the domain owner.

Google News
A news aggregate officially launched by Google in 2006. Some established
news agencies (e.g., Agence France-Presse) have requested that their articles
not be included in Google's aggregate service. However, many small domain
owners, including those that focus on the publication of branded content, often go out of their way to apply for inclusion on Google News as a way to
increase clicks and views on their site.

Misinformation
False information that is put into circulation either intentionally (see **Disinformation**) or by accident. Misinformation may include content that is false

but also content that is misleading because it is poorly researched or simply not fact-checked.

News desert
A region that has no access to daily or even weekly local news coverage. The term emerged in the early 2000s as thousands of local newspapers ceased publication in the United States and worldwide.

Participatory media
Media that depend upon the participation of users. In contrast to traditional one-to-many forms of media (e.g., a television broadcast system such as NBC or BBC), in participatory media the content is solely or primarily produced by its users. Instagram and YouTube are two well-known examples of participatory media.

Peer production
See **Commons-based peer production**.

Search engine optimization (SEO)
A constantly shifting set of strategies used by web writers and developers to ensure that their content ranks high in any search. Google has never revealed the criteria used in their Page Rank algorithm and is constantly updating the algorithm (in part, to weed out individuals and organizations attempting to game the system). As a result, SEO experts must constantly work to stay on top of their optimization efforts.

Troll factory
A type of content farm engaged in the production of disinformation or misinformation. Troll factories not only produce false or misleading content but also use a variety of strategies to ensure the content circulates widely.

User-generated content
Any content produced by users, and more specifically, content produced by online users. Common examples of user-generated content include but are not limited to videos uploaded by users to YouTube, music recordings uploaded by users to Sound Cloud, photographs uploaded by users to Instagram, and stories uploaded by users to Wattpad.

NOTES

Preface

1. Jeff Desjardins, "How Much Data Is Created Each Day?," World Economic Forum, April 17, 2019, https://www.weforum.org/agenda/2019/04/how -much-data-is-generated-each-day-cf4bddf29f/.

2. Ella Koeze and Nathaniel Popper, "The Virus Changed the Way We Internet," *New York Times*, April 7, 2020, https://www.nytimes.com/interactive /2020/04/07/technology/coronavirus-internet-use.html.

3. Quoted in Jim Turner, "'Starved for Content': Ron DeSantis Explains Why Sporting Events Are Needed Now," *Tampa Bay Times*, April 14, 2020, https:// www.tampabay.com/news/health/2020/04/14/in-defense-of-wwe-decision-ron -desantis-said-he-wants-more-sporting-events/.

4. Among other recent studies, see Jean M. Twenge and W. Keith Campbell, "Associations between Screen Time and Lower Psychological Well-Being among Children and Adolescents: Evidence from a Population-Based Study," *Preventive Medicine Reports* 12 (October 18, 2018): 271–283, doi:10.1016/j. pmedr.2018.10.003.

Chapter 1

1. Jodi Dean, *Democracy and Other Neoliberal Fantasies: Communicative Capitalism and Left Politics* (Durham: Duke University Press, 2009), 26.

2. Bharat Anand, *The Content Trap* (New York: Random House, 2016).

3. Theodor W. Adorno and Max Horkheimer, *Dialectic of Enlightenment*, trans. John Cumming (New York: Verso, 1997), 136.

4. William Safire, "The Summer of This Content," *New York Times*, August 9, 1998, section 6, p. 18.

5. John Unsworth, editor's introduction to *Postmodern Culture* 4 (2) (1994), http://pmc.iath.virginia.edu/text-only/issue.194/intro.194.

6. Joanna Brenner, "3% of Americans Use Dial-Up at Home," PEW Research Center, August 21, 2013, https://www.pewresearch.org/fact-tank/2013/08 /21/3-of-americans-use-dial-up-at-home/.

7. Adorno and Horkheimer, *Dialectic of Enlightenment*, 136.

8. Jean-François Lyotard, *The Postmodern Condition: A Report on Knowledge* (Minneapolis: University of Minnesota Press, 1979), 4–5.

9. Ibid., 5–6.

10. McKenzie Wark, *A Hacker Manifesto* (Cambridge, MA: Harvard University Press, 2006), 57–58, 26.

11. Michael Bhaskar, *The Content Machine: Towards a Theory of Publishing from the Printing Press to the Internet* (London: Anthem Press, 2013), 6.

Chapter 2

1. Kevin Killian, interview with Ruby Brunton, "Developing a Creative Process," *The Creative Independent*, March 4, 2019, https://thecreativeindependent.com/people/writer-kevin-killian-on-being-unlikeable-in-your-work/.

2. Elizabeth L. Eisenstein, *The Printing Press as an Agent of Change* (Cambridge: University of Cambridge Press, 1979), 109.

3. Oxford English Dictionary, "'Your Dictionary Needs You': A Brief History of the OED Appeals to the Public," *OED* blog, October 4, 2012, https://public.oed.com/blog/dictionary-needs-brief-history-oeds-appeals-public/.

4. Linda Kinstler, "How TripAdvisor Changed Travel," *Guardian*, August 17, 2018, https://www.theguardian.com/news/2018/aug/17/how-tripadvisor-changed-travel.

5. As cited in Ana Alacovska, "The History of Participatory Practices: Rethinking Media Genres in the History of User-Generated Content in Nineteenth-Century Travel Guidebooks," *Media, Culture and Society* 39, no. 5 (2017): 662–663.

6. Henry Jenkins, *Convergence Culture* (New York: New York University Press, 2006), 3.

7. Ibid., 259–260.

8. Yochai Benkler, "Coase's Penguin, or, Linux and *The Nature of the Firm*," *Yale Law Journal* 112, no. 3 (December 2002): 369.

9. Ibid.

10. As cited in Howard Rheingold, *The Virtual Community: Homesteading on the Electronic Frontier*, 2nd ed. (Cambridge, MA: MIT Press, 2000), 31.

11. John Perry Barlow, "A Declaration of the Independence of Cyberspace," Electronic Frontier Foundation, February 8, 1996, https://www.eff.org/cyberspace-independence.

12. Lisa Nakamura, *Cybertypes: Race, Ethnicity, and Identity on the Internet* (New York: Routledge, 2002), xii.

13. Pew Research Center, "Internet Use by Race and Ethnicity," January 11, 2017, https://www.pewresearch.org/internet/chart/internet-use-by-race.

14. Arthur Armstrong and John Hagel III, "Real Profits from Virtual Communities," *McKinsey Quarterly* 3 (1995): 2.

15. Ibid., 7.

16. Christian Fuchs, "Class and Exploitation on the Internet," in *Digital Labor*, ed. Trebor Scholz (New York: Routledge, 2013), 218.

17. Ibid., 217.

Chapter 3

1. Peter H. Lewis, "Personal Computers; Cruising the Web with a Browser," *New York Times*, February 7, 1995, C0008.

2. David Rothenberg, "How the Web Destroys the Quality of Students' Research Papers," *Chronicle of Higher Education*, August 15, 1997, https://www.chronicle.com/article/How-the-Web-Destroys-the/75214.

3. Susan Colaric and Alison A. Carr-Chellman, "Speeding on the Information Superhighway," *TechTrends* 44, no. 6 (November 2000): 28.

4. Howard Rheingold, *The Virtual Community: Homesteading on the Electronic Frontier*, 2nd ed. (Cambridge, MA: MIT Press, 2000), xxiii.

5. Robert H. Reid, *Architects of the Web: 1,000 Days That Built the Future of Business* (New York: John Wiley & Sons, 1997), 300–308.

6. In 2001, Chip Bayers reported in *Wired*, "With AdWords, an advertiser can purchase one of the small, rectangular boxes that appear to the right of the search results on selected pages for an initial fee that ranges from a $15 CPM for the top spot to $8 for the bottom four in the list of eight." Chip Bayers, "I'm Feeling Lucky," *Wired*, October 1, 2001, https://www.wired.com/2001/10/google-6/.

7. On June 18, 2003, *Wired* reported that Google was rolling out a new "self-serve program called AdSense, aimed to help operators of less-trafficked sites quickly format their Web pages to receive advertisements that match key words in the content of those individual pages." "Wired News Report," *Wired*, June 18, 2003, https://www.wired.com/2003/06/oracle-responds-with-mo-money/.

8. Daniel Roth, "The Answer Factory: Demand Media and the Fast, Disposable, and Profitable as Hell Media Model," *Wired*, October 19, 2009, https://www.wired.com/2009/10/ff-demandmedia/.

9. All the aforementioned job postings were found on Upwork.com on December 28, 2018.

10. Richard Florida, *The Rise of the Creative Class, Revisited* (New York: Basic Books, 2012).

11. Angela McRobbie, *Be Creative: Making a Living in the New Culture Industries* (Cambridge, UK: Polity Press, 2016).

12. While working on this book, I was unable to find any quantitative studies to support something I have found to be consistently true anecdotally—that

is, many people who write for content farms are graduates of either humanities programs or journalism programs. That there are no statistics tracking who works on content farms is not surprising. Since nearly all content farm work is done on a contract basis, few people who engage in content farm production are "employees" per se, making it difficult if not impossible to track who they are, their level of education, and so on. Also, most self-respecting aspiring journalists and graduates of liberal arts programs know that content farm work isn't exactly prestigious, so it is not something one necessarily wants to publicize. One doesn't need to look far, however, to find accounts that suggest much of the writing turned out on content farms is carried out by people trained in journalism and liberal arts programs; see, for example, Corbin Hiar, "Writers Explain What It's Like Toiling on a Content Farm," *Media Shift*, July 21, 2010, http://mediashift.org/2010/07/writers-explain-what-its -like-toiling-on-the-content-farm202/.

13. A longitudinal study carried out by the American Academy of Arts and Sciences found that humanities programs awarded 5,891 doctoral degrees in 2015; in 1988, when data was first collected, only 3,110 were rewarded. The American Academy of Arts and Sciences also reports that between 2000 and 2016, available jobs for people with humanities PhDs declined in all fields. For a summary of the report, see Scott Jaschik, "The Shrinking Humanities Job Market," *Inside Higher Education*, August 28, 2017, https://www .insidehighered.com/news/2017/08/28/more-humanities-phds-are-awarded-job -openings-are-disappearing.

Chapter 4

1. Erik Morse, "Amalia Ulman," *Art Review*, November 24, 2015, https:// artreview.com/features/september_2015_feature_amalia_ulman/.

2. Amalia Ulman, "Interviews," *Artforum*, May 18, 2018, https://www .artforum.com/interviews/amalia-ulman-on-her-new-book-and-internet-perfor mances-75471.

3. Pierre Bourdieu, "The Field of Cultural Production," in *The Field of Cultural Production* (New York: Columbia University Press, 1993), 42.

4. Ibid., 56.

5. Quoted in Taylor Lorenz, "Raising a Social Media Star," *Atlantic*, January 17, 2018, https://www.theatlantic.com/technology/archive/2018/01/raising -a-social-media-star/550418/.

6. Rebecca Szkutak, "How Rupi Kaur Used Instagram to Transform Poetry," Interview, October 10, 2017, https://www.interviewmagazine.com/culture /how-rupi-kaur-used-instagram-to-transform-poetry.

7. Carl Wilson, "Why Rupi Kaur and Her Peers Are the Most Popular Poets in the World," *New York Times*, December 15, 2017, https://www.nytimes.com /2017/12/15/books/review/rupi-kaur-instapoets.html.

8. Faith Hill and Karen Yuan, "How Instagram Saved Poetry," *Atlantic*, October 15, 2018, https://www.theatlantic.com/technology/archive/2018/10 /rupi-kaur-instagram-poet-entrepreneur/572746/.

9. Rumaan Alam, "Rupi Kaur Is the Writer of the Decade," *New Republic*, December 23, 2019, https://newrepublic.com/article/155930/rupi-kaur-writer -decade.

Chapter 5

1. Neil Macfarquhar, "Inside the Russian Troll Factory: Zombies and a Breakneck Pace," *New York Times*, February 18, 2018, https://www.nytimes.com /2018/02/18/world/europe/russia-troll-factory.html.

2. Anna Fifield, "Russia's Disinformation Campaign in the U.S. Has Nothing on China's Efforts in Taiwan," *Washington Post*, January 8, 2020, https://www .washingtonpost.com/world/asia_pacific/russias-disinformation-campaign-in -the-us-has-nothing-on-chinas-efforts-in-taiwan/2020/01/08/3400200a-231a -11ea-b034-de7dc2b5199b_story.html.

3. Gary King, Jennifer Pan, and Margaret E. Roberts, "How the Chinese Government Fabricates Social Media Posts for Strategic Distraction, Not Engaged Argument," *American Political Science Review* 111, no. 3 (2017): 484–501.

4. Leo Benedictus, "Invasion of the Troll Armies: From Russian Trump Supporters to Turkish State Stooges," *Guardian*, November 6, 2016, https://www .theguardian.com/media/2016/nov/06/troll-armies-social-media-trump-russian.

5. Anonymous employee, interview with author, February 18, 2020.

6. Victor Pickard, *Democracy without Journalism? Confronting the Misinformation Society* (New York: Oxford University Press, 2020), 2.

7. Ibid., 4.

8. Penelope Muse Abernathy, *The Expanding News Desert* (Chapel Hill: Center for Innovation and Sustainability in Local Media, University of North Carolina at Chapel Hill, 2018), https://www.usnewsdeserts.com/reports/expanding -news-desert/loss-of-local-news/loss-newspapers-readers/.

9. American Press Institute, "How Americans Describe Their News Consumption Behaviors," *Americans and the News Media* (2018), chapter 6, https://www .americanpressinstitute.org/publications/reports/survey-research/americans -news-consumption/.

10. Robertson Meyer, "How Many Stories Do Newspapers Publish Per Day?," *Atlantic*, May 26, 2016, https://www.theatlantic.com/technology/archive /2016/05/how-many-stories-do-newspapers-publish-per-day/483845/.

11. Pickard, *Democracy without Journalism?*, 136.

12. Dan Levin, "Why the Student Newspaper Is the Only Daily Paper in Town," *New York Times*, October 19, 2019, https://www.nytimes.com/2019/10/19/us/news-desert-ann-arbor-michigan.html.

13. See Abernathy, *Expanding News Desert*. For research on news deserts in Canada, visit the Local News Project site, https://localnewsresearchproject.ca/.

14. James T. Hamilton and Fiona Morgan, "Poor Information: How Economics Affects the Information Lives of Low-Income Individuals," *International Journal of Communication* 12 (2018): 2832–2850.

15. Elisa Shearer, "Social Media Outpaces Print Newspapers in the U.S. as a News Source," Pew Research Center, December 10, 2018, https://www.pewresearch.org/fact-tank/2018/12/10/social-media-outpaces-print-newspapers-in-the-u-s-as-a-news-source/.

16. April Simpson, "As Local News Outlets Shutter, Rural America Suffers Most," *Pew Trust Stateline*, October 21, 2019, https://www.pewtrusts.org/en/research-and-analysis/blogs/stateline/2019/10/21/as-local-news-outlets-shutter-rural-america-suffers-most.

17. Eli Pariser, *The Filter Bubble* (New York: Penguin Books, 2012).

18. Jeffrey Gottfried and Elizabeth Grieco, "Younger Americans Are Better than Older Americans at Telling Factual News Statements from Opinions," Pew Research Center, October 23, 2018, https://www.pewresearch.org/fact-tank/2018/10/23/younger-americans-are-better-than-older-americans-at-telling-factual-news-statements-from-opinions/.

19. Samantha Subramanian, "Inside the Macedonia Fake News Complex," *Wired*, February 15, 2017, https://www.wired.com/2017/02/veles-macedonia-fake-news/.

20. Charlie Warzel, "Alexandria Ocasio-Cortez Is a Perfect Foil for the Pro-Trump Media," *BuzzFeed*, January 7, 2017, https://www.buzzfeednews.com/article/charliewarzel/alexandria-ocasio-cortez-is-a-perfect-foil-for-the-pro.

21. Duncan Watts and Jonah Peretti, "Viral Marketing for the Real World," *Harvard Business Review* (May 2007), https://hbr.org/2007/05/viral-marketing-for-the-real-world.

Chapter 6

1. Siobhan Roberts, "Christopher Strachey's Nineteen-Fifties Love Machine," *New Yorker*, February 14, 2017, https://www.newyorker.com/tech/annals-of-technology/christopher-stracheys-nineteen-fifties-love-machine.

2. Angela Carr, "Jean Baudot's La machine à écrire," *Capilano Review* 3, no. 20 (2013): 94–101.

3. Keith Muscutt and David Cope, "Composing with Algorithms: An Interview with David Cope," *Computer Music Journal* 31, no. 3 (2007): 10–22.

4. Harriot Otto, "Trial of Automated News Service Underway as RADAR Makes Its First Editorial Hires," press release, PA Media Group, December 12, 2017, https://pamediagroup.com/trial-automated-news-service-underway -radar-makes-first-editorial-hires/.

5. Nicholas Diakopoulos, "Boosting Local News with Data Journalism and Automation," *Columbia Journalism Review*, January 31, 2019, https://www.cjr .org/tow_center/diakopoulos-automation-local.php.

6. BBC, "Google Funds Automated News Project," July 6, 2017, https://www .bbc.com/news/technology-40517420.

7. Jim Waterson, "Microsoft Sacks Journalists to Replace Them with Robots," *Guardian*, May 30, 2020, https://www.theguardian.com/technology/2020 /may/30/microsoft-sacks-journalists-to-replace-them-with-robots.

8. Geoff Baker, "Microsoft Is Cutting Dozens of MSN News Production Workers and Replacing Them with Artificial Intelligence," *Seattle Times*, May 29, 2020, https://www.seattletimes.com/business/local-business/microsoft-is -cutting-dozens-of-msn-news-production-workers-and-replacing-them-with -artificial-intelligence/.

9. "The Washington Post Leverages Automated Storytelling to Cover High School Football," *Washington Post*, September 1, 2017, https://www.washing tonpost.com/pr/wp/2017/09/01/the-washington-post-leverages-heliograf-to -cover-high-school-football/.

10. Nicole Kobie, "Reuters Is Taking a Big Gamble on AI-Supported Journal- ism," *Wired*, March 10, 2018, https://www.wired.co.uk/article/reuters-artificial -intelligence-journalism-newsroom-ai-lynx-insight.

11. Will Knight, "An AI That Writes Convincing Prose Risks Mass-Producing Fake News," *MIT Technology Review*, February 14, 2019, https://www .technologyreview.com/2019/02/14/137426/an-ai-tool-auto-generates-fake -news-bogus-tweets-and-plenty-of-gibberish/.

12. Estimates courtesy of Statistica's infograph, "Number of Hours of First- Run Original Content Released by Netflix Worldwide from 2012 to 2019," Jan- uary 13, 2021, https://www.statista.com/statistics/882490/netflix-original -content-hours/.

13. Wendy Lee, "Can a Computer Write a Script? Machine Learning Goes Hol- lywood," *Los Angeles Times*, April 11, 2019, https://www.latimes.com/business /hollywood/la-fi-ct-machine-learning-hollywood-20190411-story.html.

14. Ross Goodwin, *1 the Road* (Paris: Ean Boîte Éditions, 2018).

15. Brian Merchant, "Can an AI Write a Novel?," *Atlantic*, October 1, 2018, https://www.theatlantic.com/technology/archive/2018/10/automated-on-the -road/571345/

16. Elle O'Brien, "Romance Novels, Generated by Artificial Intelligence," To- wards Data Science, *Medium*, August 6, 2017, https://towardsdatascience.com /romance-novels-generated-by-artificial-intelligence-1b31d9c872b2.

17. Monica Bickert, "Charting a Way Forward: Online Content Regulation," Facebook, February 2020, https://about.fb.com/wp-content/uploads/2020 /02/Charting-A-Way-Forward_Online-Content-Regulation-White-Paper-1.pdf.

FURTHER READING

Abernathy, Penelope Muse. *The Expanding News Desert*. Chapel Hill: Center for Innovation and Sustainability in Local Media, University of North Carolina at Chapel Hill, 2018. https://www.usnewsdeserts.com/reports/expanding-news-desert/loss-of-local-news/loss-newspapers-readers/.

Adorno, Theodor W., and Max Horkheimer. *Dialectic of Enlightenment*, trans. John Cumming. New York: Verso, 1997.

Alacovska, Ana. "The History of Participatory Practices: Rethinking Media Genres in the History of User-Generated Content in Nineteenth-Century Travel Guidebooks." *Media, Culture and Society* 39, no. 5 (2017): 661–679.

Anand, Bharat. *The Content Trap*. New York: Random House, 2016.

Armstrong, Arthur, and John Hagel III. "Real Profits from Virtual Communities." *McKinsey Quarterly* 3 (1995): 126–142.

Barlow, John Perry. "A Declaration of the Independence of Cyberspace." Electronic Frontier Foundation, 1996. https://www.eff.org/cyberspace-independence.

Benkler, Yochai. "Coase's Penguin, or, Linux and *The Nature of the Firm*." *Yale Law Journal* 112, no. 3 (December 2002): 369–446.

Bhaskar, Michael. *The Content Machine: Towards a Theory of Publishing from the Printing Press to the Internet*. London: Anthem Press, 2013.

Bourdieu, Pierre. *The Field of Cultural Production*. New York: Columbia University Press, 1993.

Chen, Angela. "A Russian Troll Factory May Not Have Been Very Good at Its Job." *MIT Technology Review*, November 25, 2019. https://www.technologyreview.com/2019/11/25/131832/russia-disinformation-twitter-internet-research-agency-social-media-politics/.

Dean, Jodi. *Democracy and Other Neoliberal Fantasies: Communicative Capitalism and Left Politics*. Durham: Duke University Press, 2009.

Diakopoulos, Nicholas. "Boosting Local News with Data Journalism and Automation." *Columbia Journalism Review*, January 31, 2019. https://www.cjr.org/tow_center/diakopoulos-automation-local.php.

Fuchs, Christian. "Class and Exploitation on the Internet." In *Digital Labor*, edited by Trebor Scholz, 211–224. New York: Routledge, 2013.

Hamilton, James T., and Fiona Morgan. "Poor Information: How Economics Affects the Information Lives of Low-Income Individuals." *International Journal of Communication* 12 (2018): 2832–2850.

Jenkins, Henry. *Convergence Culture*. New York: New York University Press, 2006.

Knight, Will. "An AI That Writes Convincing Prose Risks Mass-Producing Fake News." *MIT Technology Review*, February 14, 2019. https://www.technology review.com/2019/02/14/137426/an-ai-tool-auto-generates-fake-news-bogus -tweets-and-plenty-of-gibberish/.

Lyotard, Jean-François. *The Postmodern Condition: A Report on Knowledge*. Minneapolis: University of Minnesota Press, 1979.

McRobbie, Angela. *Be Creative: Making a Living in the New Culture Industries*. Cambridge, UK: Polity Press, 2016.

Nakamura, Lisa. *Cybertypes: Race, Ethnicity, and Identity on the Internet*. New York: Routledge, 2002.

Pariser, Eli. *The Filter Bubble*. New York: Penguin Books, 2012.

Pickard, Victor. *Democracy without Journalism? Confronting the Misinformation Society*. New York: Oxford University Press, 2020.

Reid, Robert H. *Architects of the Web: 1,000 Days That Built the Future of Business*. New York: John Wiley & Sons, 1997.

Rheingold, Howard. *The Virtual Community: Homesteading on the Electronic Frontier*. 2nd ed. Cambridge, MA: MIT Press, 2000.

Roth, Daniel. "The Answer Factory: Demand Media and the Fast, Disposable, and Profitable as Hell Media Model." *Wired*, October 19, 2009.

Wark, McKenzie. *A Hacker Manifesto*. Cambridge, MA: Harvard University Press, 2006.

INDEX

Adorno, Theodor W., 5, 15–16
AdSense, 14, 62–68, 118
Advertising
  AdWords and AdSense, 14, 62–68,
    118
  automated, 13–14
  banner, 62
  and culture, 16
  and journalism, 112–113
  online, 10, 61–62
  and unique content, 66
  and websites, 62–68
AdWords, 62–63
Age of Incunabula, 58–60
Alam, Rumaan, 94
Amazon, 31–32, 55
Anand, Bharat, 4
Ancestry.com, 55
Ann Arbor, Michigan, 113
Artificial intelligence (AI), 135–136.
    See also Content automation
Arts
  and content, 82
  and cultural capital, 84
  deskilling of, 96
Automated advertising, 14
Automated script writing, 136–137

Baedeker guides, 35–36
Banner ads, 62
Barlow, John Perry, 44
Baudot, Jean, 130, 138
Benkler, Yochai, 40–42
Bertie, 134

Bhaskar, Michael, 24
Bickert, Monica, 140–142
Big data, 18
Big-seed marketing, 120–122
Black Americans, 46
Blogger, 9
Blogs, 53
Book editions, 34–35
Book trailers, 95
Bourdieu, Pierre, 82–85
Branded content, 23, 107–108
British colonies, online labor in, 76
Buzzfeed, 111

Canadian poetry, 91
Capital
  content, 85–88, 97–100
  cultural, 84, 86–87, 97–99
Career websites, 68
"Charting a Way Forward: Online
    Content Regulation," 140
China, 105
Circulation of content, 4–5, 14–15,
    131
Citizen journalism, 32
"Class and Exploitation on the
    Internet," 50
Clickbait, 58, 66–68, 71, 77
Clue, 54
"Coase's Penguin, or, Linux and *The
    Nature of the Firm*," 41
Colbert, Stephen, 117
Commons-based peer production,
    41–42

Content. *See also* Content
  automation; Content farms;
  Content industry; User-
  generated content
  as art, 82
  capturing, 37
  circulation of, 4–5, 14–15, 131
  critiques of term, 20–21
  and data, 21
  defining, 1–6, 21–22
  diversification of, 12
  educational, 24–25
  entertainment, 25–27, 135–138
  and film/TV, 26
  and information, 2–3
  journalism as, 109
  political, 116–122
  regulation of, 140–142
  search-engine-optimized, 14, 69,
    116–117
  trademarking, 6
  types of, 22–29
Content automation, 129–140
  circulation, 131
  consequences of, 139
  and entertainment, 135–138
  evolution of, 129–131
  and fake news, 134
  and music, 130
  and news deserts, 132–134
  and natural language processing,
    131
Content capital, 85–88, 97–100
Content farms, 69–78
  clickbait, 58, 66–68, 71, 77
  costs, 123
  and fake news, 78, 123
  and informed voting, 115
  and online work platforms, 73–76

and overseas labor, 76–77
and search-engine optimization,
  69
workforce, 75
and writing quality, 76–77
writing rates, 70–72
Content industry, 2, 4–22
  and circulation, 4–5
  and content literacy, 140
  and content resisters, 143
  and cultural production, 27–29
  and culture industry, 5
  defined, 14–15, 22
  factors facilitating growth,
    11–13
  factors limiting growth, 7–10
  and fake news, 123
  growth of, 7
  and journalism, 105–107, 109–
    112
  and media literacy, 116
  and news deserts, 113–115
  predictions about, 16–22
  trademarking content, 6–7
Content literacy, 139–140
Content Machine, The, 24
Content marketing, 22–23
Content resistance, 142–143
Content World Trade Show, 7
Convergence culture, 39–40, 42
Convergence Culture, 39
Cope, David, 130
Corporations, 39–40
Cosmography, 34, 38
CreateSpace, 89
Crowd-sourcing, 42
Cultural production, 82–102
  amateurs and professionals,
    96–97

content as art, 82
and content capital, 85–88, 97–99
and content industry, 27–29
and content producers, 95–96,
  100
critical reception of, 97, 100–102
and cultural capital, 84, 86–87,
  97–99
defining writers and artists, 82–83
distinctions between mediums
  and genres, 95
gatekeepers, 100–102
and Instapoetry, 93–94
and social media, 85, 88
traditional writers and artists,
  97–100
writers and artists as content
  producers, 100
Culture industry, 5, 15–16. *See also*
  Cultural production
"Culture Industry, The," 15–16
*Cybertypes: Race, Ethnicity, and
  Identity on the Internet*, 45

Data, 18, 21
Data sets, 37
Dean, Jodi, 4
"Declaration of the Independence of
  Cyberspace, A," 44
Del.icio.us, 12
Demand Media, 70
Democracy
  and monetization of politics, 119
  and news deserts, 114–115
*Democracy and Other Neoliberal
  Fantasies*, 4
Democracy without Journalism?, 108,
  113
Deskilling labor, 74, 96

Dial-up internet, 8, 11–12
Dictionaries, 35
Digital content. *See also* Content
  industry
  and circulation, 4–5
  and information, 2–3
  mobile apps, 2
  and print culture, 58–59, 95
  websites, 2
Digital divide, 45
Digital journalism, 111
Digital media, 6–7. *See also* Social
  media
Digital News Initiative (DNI),
  132
Discoverability, 11
Disinformation, 105, 107, 119, 123,
  134
Diversified content, 12
Diversity, 45–46
Domains, web, 63–64
Dove Self-Esteem Project, 23
Download speeds, 8
Dropbox, 10

E-commerce, 61
Educational content, 24–25
eHow, 57, 70
Eisenstein, Elizabeth, 34–35
Elance, 10, 13, 73–74
Electronic Frontier Foundation
  (EFF), 44
Entertainment content, 25–27,
  135–138
Excellences and Perfections, 80

Facebook, 12, 18, 38, 54,
  140–142
Facial recognition, 18, 38

Fake news, 105, 119, 123–126
  and content automation, 134
  and content farms, 78, 123
  and content industry, 123
Field of Cultural Production, The, 82
File sharing, 8
Filter bubble, 115
Fitbit, 54
Fiverr, 76
Flickr, 12
Florida, Richard, 74
Forbes platform, 106–107, 116, 134
Fox News, 54
Free content, 14
Freelancer, 76
Fuchs, Christian, 50

Genre fiction, 137–138
GeoCities, 9
Gig economy, 73–75
Global workforce, 75–77
GoDaddy, 118
Goldmann, Lucien, 83
Goodwin, Ross, 137–138
Google
  AdWords and AdSense, 14, 62–66,
    118
  content criteria, 66, 69
  Digital News Initiative (DNI), 132
  Page Rank, 104
Google Docs, 10, 13
Google News, 105–106, 124
Guru, 76

Hacker Manifesto, A, 20
Hamilton, James T., 114
Hard news, 112
Harlequin Romance, 137–138
Health-related websites, 68–69

Heliograf, 134
Hiring online, 9–10, 13
Horkheimer, Max, 5, 15–16
Hotwired, 61–62
House of Cards, 26
Humanities graduates, 75

IBM, 19, 136
Impressions, website, 64
Incunabula, 58–60
Information. *See also* Knowledge
  and content, 2–3
  control of, 17
Instagram, 54, 79, 89, 93
Instagram egg, 2–5
Instapoets, 88, 91–94
Internet. *See also* Websites; Writing,
    online
  advertising on, 10, 61–66
  commercialization of, 49
  early attitudes to, 59–60
  and racial division, 45
  speeds, 8, 11–12
  virtual communities, 43, 46–48
Internet Research Agency, 103–105
Investment knowledge, 17–18, 38
Israel Defense Force, 105

Jenkins, Henry, 39–40, 42, 147
Journalism
  and advertising, 112–113
  and branded content, 107–108
  citizen, 32
  collapse of, 108
  as content, 109
  and content automation, 132–134
  and content industry, 105–107,
    109–112
  digital, 111

local news, 113–115, 132
loss of professional journalists
    and newspapers, 108–109
news deserts, 113–115, 132–134
and news sites, 105–106
online, 113
opinion-based articles, 111–112
and troll factories, 103–105,
    107–108

Kaur, Rupi, 88–94, 100
Kelly, Kevin, 43
Keywords, 62–63
Killian, Kevin, 31–32
Knowledge. *See also* Information
    as informational commodity, 17,
    19
payment/investment, 17–18, 38
use value of, 17

Leaf Group, 70
Levine, Max, 87
Literature, 82–83, 137–138
LiveJournal, 9, 103–104
Local news, 113–115, 132
Lynx Insight, 134
Lyotard, Jean-François, 16–19, 38

Macedonian teens, 117–119
Machine à écrire, La, 130
Market economy, 27
Marketing, content, 22–23
    big-seed marketing, 120–122
    viral marketing, 121
McDonald, Kevin, 136
McRobbie, Angela, 74
Media literacy, 116, 127
Michigan Daily, 113
Microsoft, 133

Milk and Honey, 89
Misinformation, 108, 119, 123, 134
Monetization, 10, 48–49
    and fake news, 126
    of political content, 117–120
Morgan, Fiona, 114
Morse, Erik, 79–80
MSN, 133
Muirhead, John, 35–36
Multinational corporations, 18–19
Munster, Sebastian, 34, 38
MySpace, 12

Nakamura, Lisa, 45
Napster, 12
Natural language processing (NLP),
    130–131
Neoliberalism, 27–29
Netflix, 26, 135–136
News content, 95, 111, 123
News deserts, 113–115, 127, 132–
    134
Newspapers, 109, 112–115, 133–
    134
News sites, 105–106
News sources, 123–124, 126–127
New York Times, 54, 111
Non-book content, 24
Noon, John P., 6–7

Ocasio-Cortez, Alexandria, 120–
    122
oDesk, 10, 13, 73
On-Demand Publishing, 89
1 the Road, 137–138
Online communities, 43, 46–47
Online journalism, 113
Online Labor Index, 77
Online shopping, 61

Online work platforms, 73–76
OpenAI, 134
Opinion-based articles, 111–112
Organic growth, 23
Oxford English Dictionary, 35

Page views, 104
PA Media Group, 132–133
Pariser, Eli, 115
Participatory culture, 39–40
Payment knowledge, 17
Peer production, 39, 41–42
People of color, 45
PeoplePerHour, 76
Peretti, Jonah, 121–122
Performance art, online, 79–80
Pharmaceutical industry, 54–55
Philological Society of London, 35
Photographs, user, 18
Pickard, Victor, 108–109, 113
Pinterest, 105
Poetry, 91–93
Political campaigns, 120–122
Political content
  and big-seed marketing, 120–122
  content strategies, 122
  monetization of, 117–120
  search engine optimization of, 116–117
Postmodern Condition, The, 16
Postmodern Culture, 11
Powell's Books, 93
Presidential election of 2016, 108, 117–119
Print culture
  and digital content, 58–59, 95
  news outlets, 111
  word rates, 69

Print editions, 34–35
Product development and education, 25, 34
Propaganda, 124
Pro-Trump websites, 118–119
Publishing content, 23–25, 95
Publishing industry, 23–24

Racial diversity, 46
Racial division, 45
RADAR (Reporters and Data and Robots), 132–133
"Real Profits from Virtual Communities," 47
Regulation, content, 140–142
Remote work, 9–10, 13
Reproduction rate (*R*), 121
Reuters, 134
Rheingold, Howard, 60
Roth, Daniel, 70

Safire, William, 6
ScriptBook, 136
Search-engine-optimized content, 14, 69, 116–117
Search engines, 7–8, 11, 62–63
Smartphones, 14
Smith, Zadie, 137
Social media, 12–13
  as audience, 33
  and cultural production, 85, 88
  and misinformation, 108
  news feeds, 115, 124, 126
  teen influencers, 87–88
  user photos, 18
Speeds, internet, 8, 11–12
Strachey, Christopher, 129, 138
Streaming platforms, 26
Sun and the Flowers, The, 90

Talent sourcing, 41–42
Tech companies, 14
TechWalla, 70
Teen influencers, 87–88
Training industry, 25
Travel guide industry, 35–36
TripAdvisor, 35
Troll factories, 103–105, 107–108, 134
Trump, Donald, 117–118, 122, 142
Tumblr, 12, 89
TV news channel content, 95
Twitter, 12, 142

Uber, 73
Ulman, Amalia, 79–81, 85
Unregistered words, 35
Upstartle, 13
Upwork, 10, 71, 73, 96–97
User-generated content, 9, 31–55
  across media, 36–37
  as assets, 49–50
  attitudes to, 52
  classification of, 52–55
  consumers and producers, 40
  convergence culture /
    participatory media, 39–40, 42
  and corporations, 39–40
  dictionaries, 35
  and diversity, 45–46
  exploitation of, 50
  function of, 32, 54–55
  history of, 34–39
  as investment knowledge, 38
  life cycle of, 55
  and media, 53–54
  peer production, 39, 41–42
  and product development, 34
  profit from, 33, 37–38, 48–49

  promise of, 32–33
  publishing/broadcasting, 37
  travel guides, 35–36
  types of, 52–53
  and virtual communities, 43, 46–48

Varda, Agnès, 21
Video content, 95
Video files, 8
Video games, 53
Vimeo, 54
Viral marketing, 121
Virtual communities, 43, 46–48
Virtual Community, The, 60

Wark, McKenzie, 20
Warzel, Charlie, 121
Washington Post, 134
Watson, 136–137
Watts, Duncan, 121–122
WebMD, 68
Websites
  as advertising space, 62–68
  career, 68
  content of, 2
  development, 8
  and monetization of politics, 118–119, 126
  and print conventions, 59
WELL (Whole Earth 'Lectronic Link), 43, 47, 60
Whole Earth Catalog, 43
Wikipedia, 37, 52
Wilson, Carl, 90
Wired, 61, 69
Wired Ventures, 61
Work platforms, 73–76
World Wide Web. *See* Internet

Writely, 13
Writing, online
  automated script writing, 136–
    137
  pay rates, 70–72, 103
  and print culture, 59, 69
  quality of, 57–58, 60, 76–77
  and work platforms, 73–75

Xenakis, Iannis, 130

Yelp, 37, 54
YouTube, 12, 37, 54

The MIT Press Essential Knowledge Series

AI Assistants, Roberto Pieraccini
AI Ethics, Mark Coeckelbergh
Algorithms, Panos Louridas
Annotation, Remi H. Kalir and Antero Garcia
Anticorruption, Robert I. Rotberg
Auctions, Timothy P. Hubbard and Harry J. Paarsch
Behavioral Insights, Michael Hallsworth and Elspeth Kirkman
Biofabrication, Rita Raman
The Book, Amaranth Borsuk
Carbon Capture, Howard J. Herzog
Citizenship, Dimitry Kochenov
Cloud Computing, Nayan B. Ruparelia
Collaborative Society, Dariusz Jemielniak and Aleksandra Przegalinska
Computational Thinking, Peter J. Denning and Matti Tedre
Computing: A Concise History, Paul E. Ceruzzi
The Conscious Mind, Zoltan E. Torey
Content, Kate Eichhorn
Contraception: A Concise History, Donna J. Drucker
Critical Thinking, Jonathan Haber
Crowdsourcing, Daren C. Brabham
Cybersecurity, Duane Wilson
Cynicism, Ansgar Allen
Data Science, John D. Kelleher and Brendan Tierney
Death and Dying, Nicole Piemonte and Shawn Abreu
Deconstruction, David J. Gunkel
Deep Learning, John Kelleher
Extraterrestrials, Wade Roush
Extremism, J. M. Berger
Fake Photos, Hany Farid
fMRI, Peter A. Bandettini
Food, Fabio Parasecoli
Free Will, Mark Balaguer
The Future, Nick Montfort
GPS, Paul E. Ceruzzi
Haptics, Lynette A. Jones
Hate Speech, Caitlin Ring Carlson
Information and Society, Michael Buckland

Information and the Modern Corporation, James W. Cortada
Intellectual Property Strategy, John Palfrey
The Internet of Things, revised and updated edition, Samuel Greengard
Irony and Sarcasm, Roger Kreuz
Ketamine, Bita Moghaddam
Machine Learning, revised and updated edition, Ethem Alpaydın
Machine Translation, Thierry Poibeau
Macroeconomics, Felipe Larraín B.
Memes in Digital Culture, Limor Shifman
Metadata, Jeffrey Pomerantz
The Mind–Body Problem, Jonathan Westphal
MOOCs, Jonathan Haber
Neuroplasticity, Moheb Costandi
Nihilism, Nolen Gertz
Open Access, Peter Suber
Paradox, Margaret Cuonzo
Phenomenology, Chad Engelland
Post-Truth, Lee McIntyre
Quantum Entanglement, Jed Brody
Recommendation Engines, Michael Schrage
Recycling, Finn Arne Jorgensen
Robots, John Jordan
School Choice, David R. Garcia
Science Fiction, Sherryl Vint
Self-Tracking, Gina Neff and Dawn Nafus
Sexual Consent, Milena Popova
Smart Cities, Germaine R. Halegoua
Spaceflight: A Concise History, Michael J. Neufeld
Spatial Computing, Shashi Shekhar and Pamela Vold
Supernova, Or Graur
Sustainability, Kent E. Portney
Synesthesia, Richard E. Cytowic
The Technological Singularity, Murray Shanahan
3D Printing, John Jordan
Understanding Beliefs, Nils J. Nilsson
Virtual Reality, Samuel Greengard
Visual Culture, Alexis L. Boylan
Waves, Frederic Raichlen

KATE EICHHORN is a media historian and theorist. Her most recent books include *The End of Forgetting: Growing Up with Social Media* and *Adjusted Margin: Art, Activism, and Xerography in the Late Twentieth Century*. Her writing on technology, youth cultures, and education can also be found in publications such as the *MIT Technology Review*, *Wired*, and the *Times Higher Education Supplement*. She is associate professor and chair of the culture and media studies department at The New School in New York City.